WEIGHT EXPECTATIONS

of related interest

Out of the Madhouse
An Insider's Guide to Managing Depression and Anxiety
Michael Maitland and Iain Maitland
ISBN 978 1 78592 351 7
eISBN 978 1 78450 687 2

How to Kiss Goodbye to Ana
Using EFT in Recovery from Anorexia
Kim Marshall
ISBN 978 1 78592 464 4
eISBN 978 1 78450 841 8

We're All Mad Here
The No-Nonsense Guide to Living with Social Anxiety
Claire Eastham
Foreword by Natasha Devon MBE
ISBN 978 1 78592 082 0
eISBN 978 1 78450 343 7

I Can Beat Anorexia!
Finding the Motivation, Confidence and Skills
to Recover and Avoid Relapse
Dr Nicola Davies
ISBN 978 1 78592 187 2
eISBN 978 1 78450 459 5

WEIGHT EXPECTATIONS

One Man's Recovery from Anorexia

Dave Chawner

Jessica Kingsley *Publishers*
London and Philadelphia

First published in 2018
by Jessica Kingsley Publishers
73 Collier Street
London N1 9BE, UK
and
400 Market Street, Suite 400
Philadelphia, PA 19106, USA

www.jkp.com

Library of Congress Cataloging in Publication Data
A CIP catalog record for this book is available from the Library of Congress

British Library Cataloguing in Publication Data
A CIP catalogue record for this book is available from the British Library

ISBN 978 1 78592 358 6
eISBN 978 1 78450 699 5

Printed and bound in Great Britain

To Mum, Dad & Ruth

... I'm sorry

CONTENTS

INTRODUCTION

Hi, I'm Dave. Welcome to the book, it's lovely to meet you. Grab a seat, have a cuppa and make yourself at home. (Nice top, it suits you... No, really, it does.) Are you comfy? You sure? OK, I'll stop fussing.

You might be wondering who I am (don't worry, you're not the only one; my agent does too). I'm a stand-up comic. This is the book of my show *Normally Abnormal*. It's all about how I slipped into anorexia, and how I got out. Basically, it's an explanation of eating disorders from the inside looking out.

Please don't leave!!! Don't worry, this IS NOT some proper drab pity party. Eating disorders are serious, but that doesn't mean we have to be. This isn't 'Chicken Soup for the Soul' (I'm vegetarian, so that'd be wrong on so many levels). My mum always used to say, 'Life's all about the journey, not the destination.' She told me to focus on the journey and forget about the destination (which is how she lost her job as an ambulance driver). This book is fun, funny and helpful (or at least it's meant to be). It's OK to have a giggle. In fact, I'd prefer you did. When I was going through the anorexia, one of the worst things was that people began to treat me differently – like something fragile that might break at any point. That was proper isolating. People with eating disorders are just people. They're not going to bite (especially the ones with anorexia). There's no need to be scared to talk about this stuff – we all have health, we all have mental health and some of us have mental illness. That doesn't mean they're any different. You wouldn't be worried to talk to someone with a sprained ankle, so why treat someone with a mental illness differently? So, if you think you're struggling, that's OK. It's not a choice, it's not a weakness and it's not something to be ashamed of.

This is the book I wish I'd had when I didn't know anything about anorexia. All the stuff I could find was serious, clinical or seriously clinical. If I hadn't been worried before reading it, I sure-as-shit was afterwards. I didn't need a medical textbook; I just needed honesty. That's one of my biggest aims here: to be honest. And it's been bloody difficult.

Sometimes it's tempting to *massage the truth* to make the story more 'Hollywoody'. But I've tried to avoid that because I've found that the most extreme stories are the ones that get all the attention. That's because they've got the shock factor (which is like *The X Factor* only a lot more exciting). People minutes away from death, weighing less than a Styrofoam cup and looking like a human toast-rack will flog newspapers, get people watching or clicking links. However, they're not most people's experiences of an eating disorder. It's hard to tell when a social drinker becomes an alcoholic, and it's same with eating disorders. The extreme cases are just the tip of the iceberg. For every story you might see in the *Daily Mail*, there are hundreds that don't get reported because they're not 'exciting' enough. So, by being honest about my experience, I want to change that.

And being blunt, my story isn't extreme – I'd never gone days without eating, I'd never fainted or been tube-fed (unless you count Pringles). For a long time it was something I was embarrassed about – how could I consider myself anorexic if I wasn't as extreme as all these people I kept reading about? It made me feel like a failure and that kind of made it all worse. But mental illness isn't a dick-swinging contest of 'I was more ill than you'. So you won't find any mention of weights, BMI or size here – for two reasons. The first is because I'm not a cow that's being sold off at market. The second is because none of that information is important. Anorexia's a disease of the mind, not the body. It isn't about how skinny you are; it's about how much it affects you. As soon as you start moving away from numbers and start focussing on people it becomes a lot more helpful.

Which reminds me - something I want to be clear about: this isn't an autobiography. It's about my experience rather than about me. I was worried about writing this book - I didn't want it to come across as self-indulgent life advice from a middle-of-the-road comic. I'm well aware I haven't split the atom, found a cure for cancer or discovered Atlantis. So this isn't really a story about me, in the same way that *Animal Farm* isn't about some naughty pigs and *Lord of the Flies* isn't an account of a school trip gone wrong. Sometimes stories are more important than the people they happen to.

Oh, yeah, I'm a bloke! For some reason, people are always interested in that as well. A lot of people ask, 'What's it like being a man with anorexia?' but I've never been a woman with anorexia, so I don't really know how to answer that. I know some men feel it's tricky talking about this shit because eating disorders can be seen as something that affects lady-women more than men, but we're trying to change that. Illness isn't about gender: if you've got an eating disorder, you've got an eating disorder - end of! If I had tooth decay, people wouldn't be interested if I'm male or female. It's the same with eating disorders. It doesn't matter what junk you've got between your legs - eating disorders don't discriminate. So, if you're a bloke, and you think you might have an eating disorder, it doesn't make you any less of a man to go get help. You're not alone. In fact, the first recorded case of anorexia was actually a man. Surprised? Well, here's some other nifty little facts:

* *Eating disorders aren't a 'modern disease'; Mary, Queen of Scotts, Lord Byron and even people back in the 1300s can be diagnosed as anorexic.*
* *Up to 25% of anorexics are thought to be blokes.*
* *One in five young women display signs of an eating disorder.*
* *It's estimated that 6.4% of adults display signs of an eating disorder.*

This isn't *QI*, though. All I mean is that eating disorders are a big fucking deal. They're not about vanity, attention seeking or making something out of nothing. They're psychological diseases with a higher mortality rate than any other mental illness. I promise to keep it light, though (of course I will – I'm a recovering anorexic) but I just want to get across that although I might sometimes dick around, this is a big problem.

Also, I'll be honest: I don't have all the answers. I've been talking about this stuff for nearly half a decade and I still find it tricky to make sense of. There's so much crap I don't understand (if ignorance is bliss, then I've reached nirvana). I'm not a psychologist; I'm just a professional idiot. So I turned to some people who might help make sense of things. A lot of academicky human-people use this thing called the Transtheoretical Model (sounds sexy, doesn't it!). It's basically an order of phases you go through when changing behaviour. Adjustments in behaviour happen over time; they don't just go in one big jump.

The academicky science dudes reckon it happens in six stages. Have a gander if you're interested:

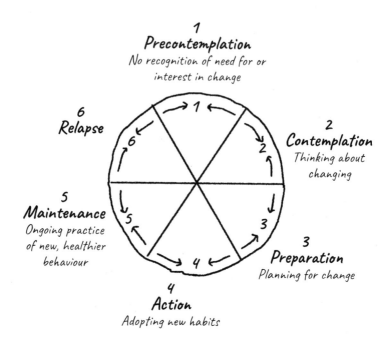

Now, all those proper intelligent people know what they're talking about. However, for me, it was a bit different. It went:

✗	Precontemplation	✗
✗	Contemplation	✗
✗	Preparation	✗
✗	Relapse	✗
✗	Action	✗
✗	Maintenance	✗

That's why I've split this up into six sections – to tell the story through what was happening at each point. At the end of each section I've given some ideas of what would have been useful for me at the time – tips to help at each of the stages. These are not medically verified; they're just some of the things I wish I'd have thought about/had at the time.

That's another thing as well: I've included music suggestions. You see, I've always wanted to write a book, so I'm really pleased you're here. I love books but there are a lot of them and a lot of good ones. I can't contend with *To Kill a Mockingbird*, *1984* and *Great Expectations*. So that got me thinking: how could I make books better? Which is why I decided to give this one a soundtrack. I'm sure I'm infringing some copyright laws, but sod it – I want my book to be fun. I've created a playlist for every section of the book. These are songs to listen along to while reading. Some of them are just tracks I was listening to at the time; others are there because they explain what I'm trying to say in a much better way than I can. Feel free to judge my music taste...everyone else does. Generally, I've got the music taste of a prepubescent girl, but I've tried to include something for everyone.

If you have any comments on my music taste, my book or just want to say 'hi', please tweet me @DaveChawner. While you're on the internet, if you want to see me in action, my website is www.davechawner.co.uk. You can also check out my TED Talk from the comfort of your own home for free. Just search 'My Battle with Anorexia – Dave Chawner' on YouTube and you should get there. If you've enjoyed it, please leave a comment. If you've enjoyed it, please recommend it. If you haven't...please keep schtum!

Now, let's sit down, have a cuppa and get comfy. It's time for you to relax; you deserve it (of course, I don't know that for certain, but you've bought this book, so in my mind that makes you one of the best humans on the planet). OK, let's crack on...and that top really does suit you!

Section 1

PRECONTEMPLATION

SONGS FOR THIS SECTION

Just Jack – Starz in Their Eyes
The Killers – When You Were Young
Gnarls Barkley – Crazy
Arctic Monkeys – Fluorescent Adolescent
Calvin Harris – Acceptable in the 80s
Foster the People – Pumped up Kicks
Kaiser Chiefs – I Predict a Riot
Klaxons – Golden Skans
The Courteeners – Not Nineteen Forever
Feeder – Feeling a Moment
Stereophonics – Nothing Precious at All
Fall Out Boy – Sugar, We're Goin Down
The Fratellis – Creepin' up the Backstairs
The View – Face for the Radio
The Pigeon Detectives – Take Her Back
The Feeling – Sewn
Badly Drawn Boy – A Minor Incident
Orson – No Tomorrow
Wheatus – Teenage Dirtbag
Sum 41 – In Too Deep
The Offspring – The Kids Aren't Alright
The Futureheads – Hounds of Love
The Pigeon Detectives – I'm Not Sorry
Empire of the Sun – We Are the People
Green Day – Basket Case
Simple Plan – Welcome to My Life
Little Man Tate – What? What You Got

Everyone says first impressions count... Why do they say that? It's hardly helpful – like your mum telling you not to look at Auntie Phil's moustache *again*. Once you're aware of something like that, it'll only make things worse. So, first, let me apologise. This story isn't dramatic. There aren't any car chases, gunfights or explosions. But the truth is, most of the time life isn't exciting. And more than anything, I want to be truthful.

This is the bit where everything began, and before I even realised something was wrong. At this point in time I didn't even know what anorexia was. I'd heard it bandied around, but didn't really understand (or if I'm honest, care) what it was. This is 'the starting point'.

'Precontemplation'
* Being unaware you have an eating disorder
* Denying you have a problem
* Defending your habits
* Being hostile if anyone suggests you might have a problem

It all begins in a sleepy little village in Staffordshire. To give you an idea of the sort of place it was, every year we held an annual scarecrow competition! It was *that* rural. We did have a gang at school, but they were called *The Scouts*. I lived just up the road from one of my best mates, Nick – I was in and out of his house so much that on more than one occasion he'd pop home to find me, his mum, dad and brother sitting at the dinner table nattering, laughing and arguing about who should do the dishes. Nick had a girlfriend, Sarah. She was quirky, cool and unknowingly one of the most popular girls in school. They'd been dating a couple of years and became two of my closest friends (and not just because they lived up the road).

I was lucky with my school and the friends I made. We all went to the most underfunded school in Staffordshire. That sounds rough, but believe me, it wasn't. We used the school's lack of budget to our advantage; when our head of Sixth Form said there wasn't enough money to decorate the Sixth Form room, our whole year clubbed together, bought paint, brushes, dust sheets and did the place up ourselves. We got a load of second-hand sofas from the YMCA, installed a stereo system, subwoofer and mid-speakers, and painted cricket stumps on the wall so we could play during free periods. It was that kind of school.

On lazy Thursday afternoons (when most of the year had free periods) we'd pootle along to the Shoulder of Mutton pub, have a couple of pints and play darts. This was only interrupted when the odd teacher would come looking for us.

Things were fun. We were only doing our AS Levels (which aren't *really* that important – they're the provisional A Levels, the dress rehearsal before the real thing). I didn't take them seriously. In fact, back then I took very little seriously. None of us did.

I was happy with my lot – things were fun. Life felt kind of like a mashup of *Friends* meets *Scrubs* meets *The O.C.* It was one of those bubble moments when I was quietly chuffed with everything and everyone. It genuinely was that good...not that I realised it, of course! Happiness is a lot like a good boss – you don't appreciate it till it's gone and you're left wondering what you're going to do without it.

Now, the reason I'm banging on about all of this is because I know stories about mental illness normally start with tragedy or horror. A lot of the time there's normally something horrific that almost *explains* why everything got a bit wonky in the upstairs department. That's not to say it's any less awful; it's just to say that there isn't really any *reason* why I became anorexic. In fact, if there had to be a reason, it'd probably be the fact that I was happy with stuff (I know, right, pity me and all my damned happiness!). There isn't one moment where this begins; it's something that happened over time, without realising. However, if I had to pick a point, it'd be 1 January 2006.

I've never been one for New Year's Resolutions. I tend to lose attention very quickly...which makes me a very bad driver. I have trouble sticking to things, and end up with a lot more ideas than actions. That Christmas I got a page-a-day diary. I decided that I'd keep a journal of my year. After all, it'd be a good way to keep track of the everything I was enjoying so much. I came up with a list of different things that I wanted to do that year. One of them was 'lose a bit of weight'. Now, I know that's hardly inventive as New Year's Resolutions go, but there was a specific reason for this.

Just before Christmas I'd been given a big role in a school play. The Drama and English department in our school was brilliant. They were the teachers everyone loved. For good reason, too. For example, the human-manchild-and-teacher Mr Bailey wrote his play *Milking the Aardvark* (something I only later realised must have been a euphemism for wanking) which was produced by human-woman-child-and-teacher Miss Cockayne (which I only later realised was quite a funny name). They'd all just done a panto called *Goldilocks and the Three Blokes*, which I'd been in with my mates Joe and Shelly. They'd been the hero and the damsel in distress...I'd been the Fairy God-mother.

Me as the Fairy Godmother in Goldilocks and the Three Blokes

Perhaps Bailey and Cockayne felt bad because they'd just given me a role as 'head bully' (something I later realised was about as suitable as casting Julian Clary in *Scarface*...is it becoming obvious how unobservant I am yet!?) in the next school play, *Sparkleshark*.

OK, stop laughing!

I know, I know, it doesn't sound like the best play in the world. In fact, it didn't turn out to be the best play in the world. It's about this teenager who sits on a roof writing stories, when, for no apparent reason, a load of people barge in on him and threaten to chuck him to his death, but he decides to write a story about a mythical dragon instead. But believe me, it was better than *Milking the Aardvark*!

In the script, it said that I had to appear topless. At that point my body was like a good cushion – plump, round and a little cuddly. None of our family were ballerinas; we came from a larger frame of humans. So I'd never really thought about body image. I wasn't vain, never spent thousands on toiletries and I only ever used hair gel once (and even then it was to give our cat Smudj a quiff). The thought of getting my doughy body out in front of everyone made me think about losing a bit of weight. It was all pretty normal: I cut out snacking, got some more exercise and watched what I ate. I did all those things that are meant to make you 'body confident'.

Looking cool! My sister and an incredibly happy Brian May lookalike (aka me)

Before I move on, there's something I want to clear up. There's a common misconception that shy people are insecure and extroverts are self-assured. That's not true. The reason I did drama wasn't because I was confident. The reason I did drama was because I was insecure, vulnerable and needy. The best defence is often a good offence, and having a 'big personality' is a good way of drowning that insecurity out. So I tried to blend in by standing out.

Which is why I grew an afro.

Don't believe me? Take a look.

In an attempt to cover up my lack of personality, I grew

ridiculous human topiary on top of my noggin. Perhaps the strangest thing about this whole story is that I was never bullied; it's ridiculous really when you think about it – I was a tubby, short kid with the body of Ronnie Corbett, the face of Adam Sandler and the hair of Oprah Winfrey. It couldn't have been easier. I'm not saying bullying's a good thing; I'm just saying I couldn't have made it any easier for potential bullies. I was like low-hanging fruit, prime for the picking on. It's something I feel guilty about when I hear stories of perfectly lovely, normal people being bullied, and here I was, a veritable Argos catalogue of bullying potential. Yet I never got a look in. So I'm sorry if you got bullied. *I* should've been bullied, not you. I was asking for it really. I just got lucky with my school and friends.

By the time *Sparkleshark* had its opening night, I'd lost a bit of weight...but no one noticed (in fairness, it's no wonder: I still had the silhouette of a human microphone). But the fact that no one mentioned my weight loss pissed me off. It was kind of like having an expensive haircut and no one noticing. So that's what I decided to do.

After the show had finished I got my head shaved.

As soon as I cut off my hair, people noticed I'd lost weight. Cutting off my hair changed my outline and made people realise I was more svelte. I was skinnier and I got compliments. Teachers, friends, even strangers complimented me. It all sounds very arrogant, but if you go around looking like a one-man Cher tribute act, anything's got to be better. Normally, the only attention I got was from people rolling their eyes from the budget Ronald McDonald they saw. Now I was getting people telling me I looked 'good'.

That was the word they used – 'good'. Over and over again. Losing weight became a way of people telling me I was 'good'. I was insecure, vulnerable and needy. Losing weight brought me

Before and after (or a convict and a Cher tribute act)

compliments, praise and attention. If losing weight was 'good', then putting on weight was 'bad'.* So surely the more weight I lost, the more gooderer I would become?

The compliments not only came from teachers, friends and strangers; they came from girls...well, a girl (singular). Still, it was amazing – a proper lady-woman had complimented me. She had breasticles and everything! I couldn't believe my luck. A real boob-laden gentlewoman said I looked good. This is something that had *NEVER* happened before. I'd always been rubbish with women. I'd been so envious of Nick and Sarah's perfect relationship that the stink of desperation came off me like sweat. The problem was, I was terrible at flirting. My only chat-up line was 'Do you come here often?' and we were at school, so that wasn't

---

*   If you want more evidence for this, you try telling someone they've lost weight; they'll probably shake you by the hand. Tell them they've put on weight and they'll probably shake you by the throat!

flirting – it was a register. Some of the jocks at school were proper pick-up artists (by which I mean they were bin men) and they used all the chat-up lines. I couldn't use them. I cocked them up. Like that time I told Annabelle, 'Nice legs, they'd look good on my floor,' or said to Sarah Brown, 'Are you a parking ticket...because you're slightly yellowish?' But here was a proper female biped who'd said I looked good. I couldn't believe it.

Let's call her Lizzie...because that was her name. I'd always had a soft spot for Lizzie; her dad had gone to school with my dad, so I'd always sort of known her...or at least *of* her. She was a year younger than me and lived at the end of my paper round. (Yes, that's right,

My thought process
* People told me I looked 'good' when I lost weight
* The more weight I lost, the better I'd look
* The better I looked, the better first impression I would create
* Back to step one

I had a paper round...I kept doing it till I was 17. Perhaps that's one of the reasons that the most female attention I'd been given up to this point was from a GP, hairdresser or teacher.) Lizzie also went to book club (OK, I went to book club as well) and was on the School Council, which I chaired (let's just overlook how achingly cool I was and move on). She was beautiful, intelligent and amazing.

She'd look at home in the pages of *Marie Claire*, whereas I'd look at home on the back of *The Big Issue*. Our paths had crossed but never overlapped. Until September that year.

Lizzie asked Shelly if I was going to the Alrewas Festival which was coming up that weekend. Even if I hadn't been before, I sure-as-shit was now. I still remember it – 23 September 2006, an evening I'd never forget.

We arrived at the festival and Lizzie came over, sat down and laid a hand on my knee. My heart skipped a beat. After 'The Lounge' [Nick, Dom and Tom's band] played I ended up going over and sitting next to her and I draped an arm over her. Next thing I know I'm taking her on a magical tour of Alrewas and we're laughing and joking. Next we're hugging each other and finally (with chants from everyone) we're kissing. A permanent smile etched on my face I find it hard to say goodbye.

That night was the start of my first ever relationship. Even though we'd kissed, spent every evening at each other's houses and went on family trips together, it still took me over two months for me to pluck up the gumption to ask her out...via text. (Yes, I know that's not what you're meant to do, but don't you remember what happened when I tried to flirt with Annabelle and Sarah Brown? I made one think I was a serial killer and the other worry she was jaundiced!) She replied, 'All right, but just don't go planning our wedding.' Which, of course, I didn't...I focussed on the honeymoon.

Lizzie lived 200 yards away from me, in a beautiful house with shiny floors. Most nights I'd pop round, have a cup of tea and watch *Grand Designs*. Sometimes we'd cook together, making pies from old recipe books her mum had forgotten about. There were nights out, nights in and everything in between. I got to know her family, friends and everything about her. I became obsessed with her because, I was...you know...falling for her (and not because of her shiny floors).

On New Year's Eve 2006 Lizzie came over. Mum and Dad were out with some friends, my sister, Ruth, was at a party in Brum, and me and Lizzie had the place to ourselves. Lying on the sofa, watching Jools Holland, drinking Lambrini was the first time it happened. I was nervous at first but also excited. I didn't know what I was doing; I'd never done it before. I'd read about how you were *meant* to do it, but reality is very different to fantasy. There was a bit of fumbling, a lot of kissing and then it happened: I told her I loved her.

She paused, looked at me and said, 'I think I love you too.' YIPPEE!

I mean, the 'think' part of that sentence was not ideal. Not many wedding vows end with 'I think'. But let's focus on the positives: she'd still *technically* said, 'I love you.' That's got to count for something. That's enough for a verbal contract, right?

She smiled, nestled into my chest and said, 'Just don't go planning our wedding.' Which, of course, I didn't...I was thinking what our kids would look like.

That night we went to a house party in town. We arrived at 11.30. As we walked through the door, a huge cheer went up. (That's not me being big-headed – I think anyone would've got a cheer arriving at that party. Even if it'd been a blood-stained, axe-wielding man-iac, they'd have at least

It's surprising that being me was OK when you look at this...but they were a bloody good bunch

got a little clap.) Everyone was there – Nick, Sarah, Joe, Shelly and most of our school – and everyone was pleased to be there. As midnight rolled around, we were all in a huge circle in the kitchen, trying (and failing) to sing 'Auld Lang Syne' while someone quietly threw up in the flowerbeds outside.

I'm not one of those blokes who enjoys being single. I've never complained about 'the ol' ball and chain' waiting at home. In fact, I hated being single and loved so many things about being in a relationship. It gave me someone to share things with; Lizzie would be the first person I'd tell when I had good or bad news. She was the person I would care for, protect and look after. She became my validation, comfort and identity. I was no longer 'Dave'; I was 'Lizzie's boyfriend'. If Lizzie had chosen me, then that meant I must be someone worth choosing. Being with her gave me a future, something to look forward to and a reason to enjoy things as they were. And the vomit-inducing thing is that at that point in time everything felt like it'd fallen into place. I'd got good friends, a great family and an amazing girlfriend. Things were pretty sweet. I know this all sounds chintzy and a bit crap, but you have to understand that things were pretty sweet back then. At that moment, being me was OK.

However, all this happiness had a time limit. As soon as everything had sorted itself out, fate was going to piss all over my cornflakes. I know I said there isn't one moment where the tone shifts, but if there was a specific point, it was at the start of 2007.

University was just around the corner. I'd chosen to go the University of Southampton. In fact, it was Lizzie's mum who was responsible for that. She was the school librarian and helped all of us with university applications. I'd originally been dead set on Sheffield Uni (the Arctic

Monkeys were big at the time and I reeeeeeeeeally wanted a South Yorkshire accent). Lizzie's mum said Southampton was great for my course. So I booked a place on the open day and decided to have a gander.

Mum, Dad and I all drove down to Southampton. We were instantly impressed by Avenue Campus – a beautiful red-brick building nestled away in the tree-lined streets opposite Southampton Common. It had a courtyard, library and tennis courts. The place felt more like CentreParcs than a university. Then we got to Highfield, the main campus. It had a babbling brook running through the heart of it, a duck pond at the bottom, library at the top and the Union pub in the middle. I decided there and then that this was where I wanted to be.*

However, that meant work. I'd dicked around so much the year before – going to the Shoulder of Mutton, doing *Sparkleshark* and playing indoor cricket – that I *really* needed to pull my finger out. Southampton needed AAB for me to get in. That was a big ask: I'd got to pretty much resit the whole AS year in Maths as well as the A Level year. Then there was English, RE, Critical Thinking, General Studies and AEA (which stands for Advanced Extension Award...and was a bit of a waste of time). In four months I'd be sitting my exams, in six months I'd be leaving school and in eight months I'd be moving away from family, friends

---

*   Disclaimer Alert: Southampton University is lovely. Southampton itself is...interesting! See the start of Section 2 for more on that.

and everything I'd ever known. If ever there was a specific turning point, this was it.

Things accelerated – deadlines, coursework, exams, essays, applications, resits. I'd bitten off more than I could chew. There was too much to do now to dick around. In fact, there was too much to do, full stop. When I was revising, I felt I should be doing coursework; when I was doing coursework, I felt like I should be doing mock exams; and when I was doing mock exams, I felt like I should know all this shit. Pretty much overnight I'd gone from happy-go-lucky to unhappy-go-go-go. There was no time to get everything done. Deadlines, coursework, exams, essays were all looming. The calendar on my wall was filled with so many red circles that it looked more like an unsuccessful game of noughts and crosses.

I wanted to hold things as they were, to make the most of everything that had just become so perfect. But I didn't have time; everything had sped up and I felt like I was being left behind.

I began missing out on all the things I'd been looking forward to – setting off rape alarms tied to balloons on the last day of school, getting drunk and playing air guitar at the final Sixth Form party, making Victoria sponge with Lizzie and bringing it to book club. There was no time for fun, only work. Deadlines, coursework, exams, essays were at the front of my mind, and at the back a realisation that if I fucked any of them up, that'd be my future screwed.

If I didn't get into university, I wouldn't be able to get a job; if I didn't get a job, I'd have to live with Mum and Dad; and if I had to live with Mum and Dad, I'd spend the rest of my life using hair gel to style Smudj's fur.

There was no time for Lizzie. It's hard to watch *Grand Designs* when you're trying to remember how to do binomial expansions. We'd try to make pie together, but that just made me think of geometry. Even her shiny floors made me think of reflecting the x-axis on the y-axis. It was like my brain had too many tabs open. I was always thinking of something else, never fully in the moment, which made me distant and push Lizzie away. I wanted to see her as much as possible, make the most of the time we had before I moved away, but I also had coursework, exams, essays. In four months I'd be sitting my exams, in six months I'd be leaving school and in eight months I'd be 150 miles away, leaving her behind. Exams and that were all I could think about. I became continually anxious. We tried to find quality time together, but with time running out it put pressure on every moment. I was scared of losing her, but I was also scared of failing my exams, fucking up my life and styling my cat's hair for the rest of my life. She'd got her own exams too, and things between us changed. Our relationship wasn't the same anymore; we could both feel it but neither of us could explain it. That unspoken tension pushed us apart and eventually we broke up.

I was devastated.

Now, I know this sounds very Richard Curtis, but life isn't like it is in the movies. And more than anything, I want to be truthful with you. If I was Hugh Grant, I would have got drunk, done something hilarious and won back the girl of my dreams. But I'm not Hugh Grant, I didn't have time to get drunk and I didn't win her back. We broke up, she moved on and I felt trapped. It was my first love and I didn't deal with it well. The break-up with Lizzie left me feeling a lot of things - rejected, stupid and angry. It felt unfair. Everything had been so perfect and now it'd all been shot to shit. As soon as I got the girl of my dreams, I also got lumped with the most important exams of my life, followed by the prospect of moving away and having to start my life afresh at uni. I was bitter and angry that things couldn't have just worked out. I was insecure that I'd never find anyone like her ever again - that was a comforting thought! I was sorry for myself - that she was 'the one that got away' - but I was also nervous about the future. I'd had so much stability with my friends, family and Lizzie, but that was about to change. Everything felt so uncertain.

Now, I realise I didn't go through anything special. I'm not first person to be dumped - people get ditched every single day and get on with it. I'm not the first person to go to university either, and I'm definitely not the first teenager to have angst. To be honest, that's something I feel really guilty about - people have so much worse crap to deal with and cope much better than I did. But that was my problem: I didn't really know how to cope with all that change, angst and pressure. It acted as a 'trigger'.* One thing I want to be absolutely clear about is that Lizzie didn't cause my anorexia. It was (partially) stoked by my inability to deal with change. I'd loved everything how it was and I wanted to go back to when everything'd been perfect. Anorexia became a way of coping, a subliminal response to my situation. It didn't 'begin' so much as 'develop', and it crept up gradually, like an annoying itch on the back of your hand. I didn't know what I was doing; behaviours just kind of developed without my realising, and I thought they were all helping me get back on top of things.

For example, I began weighing myself in the morning. Ever since I'd wanted to lose weight for *Sparkleshark*, I'd been weighing myself every now and then, to keep track of things. However, now it was different. Weight became something to obsess over, to distract me from everything I didn't want to think about. I became increasingly preoccupied with my weight and found it fluctuated throughout the day. That scared me as it was yet another thing that I wasn't on top of. However, it was also something that I could control. I started weighing myself before I went to bed to give me an idea of how much I'd put on during the day. Then I began popping home at lunch to have a little check on the scales to see if my weight had gone up or down. This either motivated me to lose more or

---

*   Basically, a 'trigger' is psychology talk for an event/situation that causes a mental reaction.

shamed me into eating less through the afternoon. All this was a nice distraction from exams, essays and deadlines. It was like a little game I played with myself – kind of like *Play Your Cards Right*, but with weighing scales rather than cards. Losing weight became a shortcut to feeling good. Every time the needle dropped lower, it was a little win – I was hitting targets, achieving goals, in control. It was great to have something that made me feel better, a little pick-me-up. I began to associate losing weight with feeling good. Let's not forget I'd just been dumped, was resitting exams and applying to (and getting rejected by) universities – feeling good was something increasingly uncommon. That's not to mention that the more weight I lost, the more people told me I looked 'good'. This repetition built up a pattern in my mind: it seemed obvious the more weight I lost, the better I'd feel. I told myself things would improve and I could finally get back on top of life.

As weight became increasingly important, so did food. I'd never really thought about what was in my food before. We'd done nutrition in biology, but that'd been as exciting as playing chess with a vacuum. I began reading the nutritional information on the backs of packets and realised so much of the food I loved was filled with calories (of course it is!). But I became obsessed by it. For example, two pints of Fosters has more calories a McDonald's Cheeseburger! I went online, Googled 'Calorie Counters', bought books, picked up leaflets, became an expert on reducing my calorie intake. Mealtimes became maths equations. I'd try to tot up the calories on the plate. At family meals I'd be distracted trying to do the mental arithmetic while trying to keep track of the conversation. This began to spill over into day-to-day life. When I was walking home to weigh myself, I'd add the calories from that coffee, that banana, that apple. To be safe, I'd exaggerate the value of each. For example, I'd count bananas as 150 calories (even though they're only about 90). That way, I had a buffer to stop me from overeating.

As I became more obsessed with calories, I became less trusting of food. I'd read an article about companies printing much lower calorie counts on their packets than there were in the actual products. This built up a paranoia around food. I began to only eat what I'd prepared, so that I knew what went into it.

I began lying about what I'd eaten. I'd tell Mum and Dad I'd had dinner before they'd got in. I'd leave empty wrappers lying around my room to avoid awkward questions. I'd take food for lunch and throw it in the bin at school. I'd chew leftovers in front of people and spit it out in the kitchen when no one was around. I became a bloody ninja at making people think I was eating.

Then food rituals began to develop. I'd reduce portion sizes, eating off small plates to make the small servings appear bigger. I'd go to the toilet before every meal, so I was completely empty. I'd wash my hands thoroughly, so that I was completely clean. I'd switch my phone on to airplane mode, so no one disturbed me. I'd only eat with my special cutlery, drink out of my special glass and at my special table place. Everything had to be perfect; eating without the food rituals felt like a wasted meal. If a meal was wasted, I'd feel disgusted. I'd try to make myself sick. (I could never do it – I tried numerous times and it pissed me off more each time. How do bulimics do it!?)

I became obsessed with exercise. It started off as sit-ups when I woke up. I'd do blocks of 20 of them before weighing myself. Then I decided to introduce push-ups, in blocks of 25. After a while I began doing squats. I started doing this in the evening as well as the morning. Eventually, I started doing it when I came home at lunch to weigh myself. Mum and Dad realised something was up, but when I later asked them why they never said anything, my mum told me, 'When your teenage son keeps on running up to his room, and all you can hear is rhythmical banging followed by repeated grunting, you tend not to ask questions!' They must have thought I was a bloody sex pest, jogging home twice a day just to have a wank.

But the exercise wasn't only in my room. I'd create excuses to go on hour-long walks every evening. I took up running once, twice, three times a week if I could. I'd go swimming, doing 50 laps at a time.

Of course, there were the people telling me I had a problem. But the words they used were too dramatic to describe what I was doing. There were two main reactions.

THE HOLLYWOOD

* Screaming, shouting and lots of melodrama. For 'The Full Hollywood', expect tears, slamming doors and smashed crockery. This tactic is normally in a domestic setting.
* The Hollywood is born out of frustration and uses drama to try to shock as its primary tactic.
* Phrases associated with The Hollywood: 'You're wasting away', 'You're killing yourself', 'This has to stop'.

THE MOUSE

* This is the opposite of The Hollywood: whispers, hushed conversations and 'private chats'.
* This is normally initiated by 'going for a coffee' or 'having a word'. This approach appeals to sensitivity and uses emotion as its motivator.
* Phrases associated with The Mouse: 'I'm worried about you', 'Talk to me', 'What's going on?'

Both approaches were too much. This wasn't Hollyoaks! If people were going to treat this as one big melodrama, it was their problem, not mine. What I was doing wasn't an issue; it was enjoyable – my private little game. When I was restricting, exercising and losing weight, I loved it. I could give it up whenever I wanted...I just didn't want to. Not yet.

I'd give up when I got down to my next target weight. I'd give up when my trousers didn't fit. I'd give up when I didn't enjoy it... But the problem was I never wanted to. You see, none of this was really about weight, calories or exercise; it was really about achievement. With so many big scary hoops to jump through, managing my weight, calories and body was *achievable*. It was a distraction from the anxiety of exams, the fear of leaving and the loneliness of the break-up. I used my body to show there was something wrong with my mind. I wasn't really conscious I'd made this decision at the time. It was something that developed out of nothing. It all seems clear when written down, but it's taken time, effort and hindsight to wrap my head around. Back then it was just a jumble of emotions. Everything was too intense and disorienting. I didn't know this was 'abnormal' (whatever that means!) – how would I? You can't compare your mind with anyone else's. Asking if this behaviour was unusual is like asking if I see red in the same way that Gordon Ramsay does (something no one will ever know, because Gordon Ramsay can only swear when he sees red). I had nothing to compare my experiences with, so how in hell's name was I going to know something was out of whack?

If I'd have got help then, this would be a very different story (and a much shorter story too!). But I didn't think I had a problem. It's hard to tell when a couple of drinks becomes an issue, and it's even trickier to tell when 'getting healthy' becomes unhealthy.

So I rejected people's fears, carried on getting ready for uni. Life doesn't stop for mental illness and neither did I. It wasn't all doom and gloom, though. We had fun. Like the pranks on the last day of school, the time our whole year went out to Balti Towers, Katy Honeybourne's House Party (where Sam Miles had his first ever drag on a cigar...and nearly choked to death) and a holiday in St Ives with Nick and Sarah. It was a bloody good summer, and, yeah, I didn't want it to end, but you know what? Life goes on. Maybe it'd even be better. After all, everyone kept telling me uni would be the best days of my life. It was a pretty big claim; uni had a lot to live up to and although I wasn't ready to leave, I was about as ready as I'd ever be.

TIPS TO HELP AT THIS STAGE

Diary

Since I started that diary back in 2006, I've kept one every day right up to now. I can't recommend it enough. However, I do have some tips:

- Write as if it's going to be read – that way you protect yourself and other people. There's a paranoia someone might secretly read your diary or fear someone's going to read something horrible you've written about them. It's good practice (in life, not just in a diary!) not to do that.

- Be positive – no one wants to read a moping dirge. That's not to say you shouldn't be honest. Phrases like 'It's so hard being me' might make you cringe. Finding the funny in situations will make it much more fun to write and a hell of a lot more enjoyable to read.

- Perspective – your future self might be reading this. That helps put things into perspective. The day-to-day worries of money, deadlines and jobs normally tend to fade over time and you remember the important stuff. Remembering that things will sort themselves out somehow is not only comforting but also really helpful.

- Read – don't forget to read back through your old diaries. Who knows, you might be impressed with how you dealt with something, how someone helped you or what you didn't know back then. Reading back old diaries is a great way of motivating you to keep going.

- Keep at it – writing a diary every day can be intimidating prospect, but it doesn't have to be. Everyone works in different ways; keeping a diary is one way of finding out how you work best. You could write a couple of entries at a time, maybe write about the morning in your lunch hour and about the afternoon before going to bed. Experiment and see what works for you. It's good discipline too.

- *Find your inner writer – dick about with different writing styles. Write your day through someone else's perspective, as if you're a character in a book or in the style of Charles Dickens! Find out what works for you and be creative about it.*

Personality tests

How many times have you heard the phrase 'just be yourself'? What the fuck does that mean?! That's like screaming 'DON'T PANIC!' I didn't/don't/perhaps never will know what it means to just be yourself – who I am, how I react and what I say changes based on my mood, situation and circumstance. Sometimes I'm sociable; sometimes I'll stare at my phone to avoid everyone and everything. What I needed was a starting point. So I took a personality test. There are loads online like the Myers–Briggs test, the Minnesota Multiphasic Personality Inventory and loads of other ones. I don't think they're a great place to go for answers, but I think they're a bloody brilliant place to go for inspiration. They could flag up things that you might be good at that you'd never thought about, or help to explain some less favourable parts of your personality. Plus, you lost nothing by having a go.

Be your own movie

This isn't my idea (even though I wish it was). An amazing girl once told me whenever she felt overwhelmed and 'stuck inside her own head', she'd imagine the movie of her day. So, if her day was a Hollywood film, what would it look like? She'd think about the actors she'd use, the soundtrack she'd play and the voice-over. I love this idea. Basically it's a distraction technique, but what a bloody brilliant one! It works for me because I don't have an internal monologue – I'm not very conscious of what I am thinking. I don't think in words, so my thought process isn't that conscious. That's why I like talking, because a lot of the time I don't know what's in my head until it comes out of my mouth! My thought process is much more emotional. The problem is emotions are hard to decipher – anxiety is very close to excitement, for example. So, sometimes, actually narrating what I'm doing is quite helpful. Obviously, it's best to do it under your breath (otherwise you get a few strange looks!) but it does work.

Music
I remember, at this time, one of the most useful things I had was music. That's why I have created a playlist at the start of each section. Music has a unique ability to reach. Whether that is listening to, playing or singing along to it.

Take yourself on a date
Right, I know this sounds wanky, but this is actually one someone else told me. A lot of the time when you are dating someone, you do all of those things that you have been saving up – going to see that play, visiting that place

and trying something new. Being single is cheaper, so use that money on you! Go on a spa day, go on a rally driving course...go on whatever you want.

Experiment

Now I've got to be careful what I say here. I'm not condoning drug, drink or substance misuse. What I am saying is, you're only young once, so don't waste that opportunity to experiment. Maybe you're a guy who likes wearing eyeliner, maybe you're a girl who likes shaving her head, maybe you are trans and want people to know. Whatever it is, muck about, find out who you are and be prepared to get it wrong. Do you remember Joe (from 'Goldilocks and the Three Blokes')? He is one of the best people at this. He wore bowling shoes for a year, went to India for six weeks alone when he was 20 and trained as a doctor, only to qualify, realise that's not for him and then begin a film-making course. When I was a teenager, I was so preoccupied with getting things right that I never really considered what it was that I wanted to get right. Part of the fun of being a teenager is you can dye your hair, change your wardrobe and listen to whatever the fuck music you want and people will think it's OK because you're a teenager. Don't waste that. At any other time in life, people will chalk that up as a 'mid-life crisis' and say you're sad for it. Experiment. See what works. Laugh at what doesn't. But no matter what you do, make sure you're safe.

Feel-good folder

On my phone I've got a folder full of silly, fun and funny photos. When things get a little intense, it's good to know they're there. I've got YouTube playlists of songs that pick me up, a drawer full of old birthday cards, ticket stubs and lanyards from festivals I've done.

Karma yourself

Perhaps there isn't such a thing as a completely selfless deed, but you know what, that doesn't have to be such a bad thing. If you can help someone and it helps you in the process, then surely everyone's a winner. Everyday acts of kindness can help make you feel like a better person, and when you feel like a better person, you can start to enjoy being you more. There are loads of little things you could do – write a note to a stranger and put it in a library book, pay someone a genuine compliment, offer up your seat on the train or bus. Make other people feel better and make yourself happier in the process.

Make yourself laugh

At that time, I began taking things too seriously. The best way to remove yourself from seriousness is to laugh. Build up a bank of YouTube videos that make you laugh, have a collection of DVDs that make you chuckle, quotes that you find funny, pictures that'll crack a smile – anything.

Get out!

One of the best releases back then was going for a drive. I bloody love driving – the freedom, the control, the comfort. If you can't drive, or don't have a car, what about cycling? If you can't drive or cycle, what about going for a walk?

Section 2

CONTEMPLATION

SONGS FOR THIS SECTION

Marina and the Diamonds – I Am Not a Robot
Vampire Weekend – A-Punk
La Roux – Bulletproof
Kate Nash – Foundations
The Wombats – Moving to New York
The Hoosiers – Goodbye Mr A
Scouting for Girls – She's So Lovely
The Ting Tings – That's Not My Name
The Strokes – Last Nite
The Automatic – Monster
Lady Gaga – Poker Face
Jason Mraz – I'm Yours
The Fray – How to Save a Life
The Black Eyed Peas – I Gotta Feeling
Rilo Kiley – Portions for Foxes
Owl City – Fireflies
Gabriella Cilmi – Sweet about Me
Ben Folds – Rockin' the Suburbs
Alphabeat – Fascination
Carly Rae Jepson – Call Me Maybe
Gotye – Somebody That I Used to Know
Jack Johnson – Good People
Duffy – Warwick Avenue
Robyn – Dancing on My Own
Mark Ronson – Valerie

This is when I began to realise something might've gone a bit wonky...but it wasn't a big deal. After all, I wasn't 'fully' anorexic like those women in magazines, I didn't have bones jutting out, I wasn't fainting or anything. What I was doing was just a bit...unusual!? Could you call it eccentric? It was a bit like a teenager who wears a bow tie - odd but not full-on mental. It was more of a hobby than an 'illness'.

Every now and then I'd think I might need to do something, but I never really got round to it. 'Getting help' was a bit like organising my sock drawer - something I should do, but I kept putting it off because I didn't really know where to start. I made little promises to myself, like I'd get help when I got down to my next target weight, or when I began having problems, at the end of the month/at the end of the year/at the end of the century, when there wasn't a 'y' in the day. Truth is, I didn't really know what 'getting help' meant. If I told my friends I was having problems eating, they'd probably stare blankly and tell me to 'put food on your fork and then lift it to your mouth'. If I went to a doctor, he'd ask what was wrong. How the fuck do you even start to answer that question? It was more of a feeling, a lacking, an awareness that I wasn't really coping. How do you explain that to a doctor? I couldn't even explain it to myself, let alone some imposing bloke/blokette sporting a white coat and stethoscope. The only question worse than that'd be 'What would you like me to do?' I hadn't got a frigging clue what I wanted the doctor to do - ideally, I wanted him to take this all away, take me back to the Fun Dave I'd enjoyed being and give me a million quid. But unless he had a time machine, omniscient powers and some dodgy funding, there was no way that was going to happen.

My anorexic voice was always buzzing round like an annoying wasp – I had the choice to ignore it or try swatting it away (which means disrupting everyone and making the people that can't see it think you're mad). Sometimes I'd realise this'd all probably only get worse, which wasn't ideal, but that was Future Dave's problem (along with my overdraft, student loan and employment prospects).

'Contemplation'

* You think there might be a problem
* Think about changing...but don't do anything about it
* Wonder what things would be like if you did change

Before moving to uni, everyone told me these were going to be 'the best days of your life'. That's lovely and all that...but it's a shit-tonne of pressure! It's like telling someone first impressions count (and we've already agreed that's a bloody stupid thing to do!). I chose to go to Southampton Uni for three reasons:

1. I liked the course.
2. The campus was bootiful.
3. It had a beach.

I didn't check this last one, but I didn't have to. We all know, everywhere on the South Coast has to have a beach. It's one of those weird by-laws, like it's illegal to eat a pregnant woman and a swan can wee in a policeman's helmet. I'd been watching loads of *The O.C.* before going to uni and thought the South Coast of England was pretty much exactly the same as California, only a little bit further right on the map. I'd imagined beers on the beach, skinny dipping and revising over barbecues in the summer (which is a silly thing to do: the paper would catch fire and then you'd have no notes and third-degree burns – so never revise over a barbecue).

Spoiler Alert: Southampton has no beach. In fact, Southampton doesn't have a lot of things – a heart, a soul or any civic pride. I don't like bad-mouthing places; I think it's lazy and offensive. However, I'll make an exception for Southampton. The place used to be proper nice in Georgian times but then little ol' Hitler decided to shell the shit out of it during the Second World War (because it was a major port and the place they built Spitfire planes). So they had to build pretty much everything again after the war and now the place is a concrete jungle which looks like one giant sewage treatment plant. The main nice thing about Southampton is it has loads of open spaces and green parks...but it says something about a place when it's main selling point is that there are areas where people haven't fucked it up building eyesores. Poor Southampton hasn't really got a lot going for it. In fact, the year I left they built an IKEA and the locals went batshit crazy. It was like they'd just found a disused gold mine – there was a grand opening with balloon modellers, stilt walkers and a marching band. It was the biggest local attraction since Asda built a car park (and they had a 21-gun salute, a military fly-by and a royal visit to celebrate that!).

But I didn't know any of this before I went to Southampton. In my mind, I'd imagined moving away from home, being independent and settling in to my new life as a proper-grown-up-human-adult-person. I'd no longer be living with Mummy and Daddy; I'd be moving on, moving up in the world. I'd have my own 'crib', a bachelor pad, a man-cave. I was going to have somewhere cool to live.

Another Spoiler Alert: I did not have somewhere cool to live. My hall of residence wasn't some 'cool new digs' – it was more of 'a dirty dive'. It had a lot of people and very few amenities: four showers, two ovens and one microwave between 22 of us. Plus we were all self-catered – at least prisoners get their food cooked for 'em! With 22 people sharing a kitchen, mealtimes were like UN food drops. The one bin we shared in the kitchen would fill up quickly, and instead of cleaning it out, people played what was later known as 'Bin Jenga' where you had to try to balance your rubbish on the existing heap of waste; if it fell over, then you had to take the bins out. Put it this way, I was sharing a microwave with more people than I'd shared a class with at school.

The rooms were small and with very few home comforts;

you got a bed, a wardrobe and a desk. There was a little noticeboard, the sort you'd get in a GP's waiting room, and the only bit of 'personality' in the room were the fire safety instructions which were 40 years old, yellowing and peeling at the corners. I'd unadvisedly gone for the cheapest room-type in the whole block. The biggest difference there, was that it had a communal wash area, meaning I had to share a sink – I literally couldn't sink any lower (oh, come on, that's funny!). The place was one level above squatting!

My sink-mate was a six-foot boxer called Sean from South London. He was studying History and liked listening to 'Eye of the Tiger' at full blast at 3am. Sean understood as much about personal hygiene as he did string theory. He used to leave a constantly damp shaving sponge on the side of the side of the sink, which began to become mouldy and caused us to fail our room inspection. His reaction was 'OK, it *is* mouldy, but it's *my* mould'. The problem was, it wasn't *his* mould, it was *our* mould. So I'd moved to university to share a microwave with 22 people I didn't know, play 'Bin Jenga' on a daily basis and go halves on a sink with a six-foot-tall boxer who was possessive about his mould. There's nothing like home comforts to stop you feeling homesick... and this was nothing like 'home comforts'.

At least it was fresh start, though – a clean break, a blank canvas, an opportunity to rattle off ridiculous metaphors. No one knew me and I could be whoever I wanted. I could road-test a new nickname, something like 'Knuckles' or 'Jimmy the Hat' (or perhaps even something that didn't make me sound like a 1930s American gangster). I could get a new hairstyle (definitely *not* an afro!), I could adopt a new accent, I could regret that new accent, revert to my old accent, try to make people forget the new accent happened in the first place. In short, the possibilities were endless. Possibilities for excitement and possibilities for regret. It was a new place, with new people and a new start.

Now, don't get me wrong, I like meeting new people, but you can have too much of a good thing. New people were everywhere – new people on my course, new people in halls, new people on nights out. You'd open the kitchen cupboards and new people came toppling down on you, you'd turn on the shower and new people would come flowing out – it was like the zombie apocalypse (only with new people). Where were all these new people coming from?! It was all exciting and that, but it was also bloody overwhelming. Going to loud clubs, staying up till 3am and getting off your nut on snakebite is fun once in a while, but that was every friggin' night. Plus we had Freshers *Fortnight* so the onslaught carried on for 14 days! It was like a stag do, and they can be fun, but no one goes on a stag do in order to relax and feel energised. I didn't want to go out and get smashed, I just wanted to know people and have fun. Being constantly surrounded by new people who are (seemingly) having a great time is one of the most isolating experiences I've ever had. You feel like the odd one out, like the only person not having a ball and revelling in your new-found 'freedom'. On top of all of this, I had the memory of people telling me 'these will be the best days of your life'. If this was me at my peak, the rest of my life was going to be shit!

OK, you might think I'm being a grumpus, and you're kind of right. The truth is things weren't really that bad; it was all just a bit overwhelming, that's all. I didn't deal with the transition well. I found it hard to adjust...and I hated that, as it made me feel a little bit pathetic. I wanted something familiar to cling to...which is how our old friend 'restriction' comes back in the picture. It wasn't a conscious decision and it didn't happen overnight, but it was something I eventually crept towards again. Back home, when I'd begun restricting, everything had got better - people told me I looked 'good', I started dating Lizzie and everything had fitted into place. I associated restriction with success, comfort and things getting better. And no wonder I did. It deadened all my anxiety, worries and fear about the future. I was burying my problems - it wasn't a solution, but it was a way of coping. Restriction was something I could manage when everything else felt proper unmanageable. Without Mum and Dad breathing down my neck, I could get away with restricting more than ever before. It was great. And with so many people in the flat, I could go for days without eating and no one would notice (not that I actually could, of course - I was more of a 'little and unoften' kind of guy). Restriction also helped deaden the feeling of loneliness. Now, I know I've dropped 'The "L" Bomb' so I'm going to have to explain. So buckle up.

If I'm honest, I don't like the word 'lonely'; it sounds all pitiful and that. It evokes pity and *I do not want pity* (if I wanted you to feel sorry for me, I'd just show you my bank balance). Loneliness is one of those words that can mean different things to different people at different times. The loneliness I'm talking about here's not the last-guy-to-be-picked-for-the-football-team kind; it's the empty, hollow, meaningless kind.

OK, I've got to backtrack here a little bit. I should've explained, one of the reasons I took the break-up with Lizzie so badly was because I always felt like the last guy stranded on earth. Even with lots of people round me, I still felt lonely and disconnected somehow. I could hang out with people and see them party, but it was almost as if I was watching it through plate glass. It was like I was lacking something. Being 'Lizzie's Boyfriend' gave me a title, a responsibility and an identity. It gave me something to 'be'. It defined me. And without that I felt empty.

I didn't know how to get that stability back. One thing was certain: Lizzie would never take me back. The last time I'd properly seen her was at a house party when she'd been snogging some guy's face off. I'd tried to convince myself she was giving him mouth-to-mouth resuscitation, that it was her First Aid Training coming into action. But there definitely was some action happening, and it wasn't to do with first aid. Their arms had been flailing around like an octopus trying to do charades. Now, I'm not proud of this – it was wrong, silly and immature – but I gave the guy a bit of a hard time. Basically, I acted like a bit of a dick. After all, he was cooler than me, more popular and in a band (which had some wanky name like 'Hot Buttered Chaos' or 'The Weasel Destroyers'). Truth be told, I was jealous and I'd been hurt. I now realise I didn't really want a girlfriend: I wanted someone to validate me, to make me to believe in me and make me less lonely...that still doesn't excuse the fact that I was a bit of a prick that night.

So, with me and Lizzie never getting back together, perhaps I'd find someone at university? After all, the place was overrun with new people so it should be easy, right? Let's not forget, I am *terrible* with flirting (remember how I told Annabelle that she'd got nice legs and they'd look good on my floor!?). I never went 'on the pull' – people like Sean (my six-foot-tall sink-mate) put me off. He once told me the benefits of 'negging' girls (where you basically try to grind their self-confidence down to a pulp and then swoop in to make them feel better by telling them, 'But don't worry, I'd shag you' – like they're meant to turn around and say, 'Oh, thank you very much, lead the way to your boudoir, kind sir'). He treated nightclubs like a human zoo, looking to track down the vulnerable gazelle that'd become separated from the pack. Sean would track his prey, round them off and go in for the kill (not actual murder, of course – I just got carried away with the metaphor). He'd ask if he could get her a drink and then take her back to his mouldy-sink-sponge lair for strangely aggressive sex.

I didn't want to be associated with that kind of guy. If I went up to a girl and asked to buy her a drink, I didn't want her to think that it would be one part vodka, two parts coke and three parts Rohypnol. I was so worried about not coming across as rapey that I camped it up so that I didn't come across as a threat. I always felt testosterone-fuelled fellas were just looking for somewhere to put their dicks. I never wanted women thinking I was 'one of them guys' just trying to get into their pants. I really wasn't (I'd never want to get into a girl's pants – I once tried on a thong and it was like dental floss tied over a bean bag). I wanted to be thought of as more than just a penis on legs, so I became camp to try to distinguish myself from the cock-jocks. However, it kind of backfired: most girls thought I was gay.

Also, let's not overlook the fact that flirting opened me up to rejection. Even if I did pluck up the gumption to find a nice lady-woman and tell her I thought she was visually delightful, then she'd definitely turn me down. Not only because no one uses the term 'visually delightful' but also because I was going based purely on her looks. There's a very fine line between telling someone they look good and objectifying them. The problem is, all flirting is based on appearance. I worry that means I'm objectifying women like some farmer in a cattle market. Believe me, I've tried to flirt without mentioning appearance and it doesn't work. I've tried to be all feministy about it, but girls just thought I was weird asking, 'Hey girl, are you tired? Because you've been working 15% harder for 20% less money.' Or, 'Hey girl, did it hurt when you fell and smashed the glass ceiling?' Truth is, I couldn't flirt because I worried too much about what people thought. Add my insecurities about being rejected on to this and you've got a cherry on top of a very large gooey insecurity-cake.

With flirting out of the question, finding a girlfriend felt completely out of my control. Being too insecure and worried about how to approach women, I had to wait for them to approach me. That might sound very progressive and 21st century of me, but it never happened. Not once. Not even nearly. It just meant I became cripplingly self-conscious. After all, if I wasn't going to approach women, the only thing I could do to attract them was increase my chances of being seen. I wasn't tall, dark and handsome, I couldn't do anything to develop a chiselled jaw, but I could do something about my weight. Let's not forget, I'd found my last girlfriend after I'd lost weight, so if I lost more weight, that'd lead me to another girlfriend, which would help me get over Lizzie and lead to long-term happiness. Simples!

This leads me to one of the trickiest parts to explain: the relationship between anorexia and body image. I've got to be really careful what I say here because I don't want to say anything wrong. You've got to remember that the only experience I can talk about is my own. So, I can't talk for anybody else. I'm very aware that there are people out there who think anorexia doesn't really exist – that it's about wanting to look skinny and sexy, or a vanity project gone wrong. I don't want to have a go at those people. In fact, those are the people I want to try to reach. Why? Well, I understand that, from the outside looking in, all this stuff must seem bloody frustrating and very self-absorbed:

there are kids starving in the world without food and clean water, and here I am refusing to chuck anything in my gob. It seems sort of selfish to moan about how terrible it was for me being all hungry and that, when there are kids in the Third World who don't have a grain of rice to chomp on. I was aware of that. I thought about that every day. In fact, I still think about that and I still feel *fucking* guilty. I know it seems privileged, but the truth is my anorexia wasn't about trying to look sexy. Losing weight was more about blending in than it was about standing out. I'd been a chubby, awkward, self-conscious schoolboy trying to grow up to be a man. I didn't really know how to get rid of the awkwardness or self-consciousness, but I did know how to get rid of the chubbiness. Perhaps if I thinned down a bit, that'd make me less self-conscious because I wouldn't stick out as much. So, my anorexia was (at least partly) about how I looked, but it wasn't about vanity. It was more about trying to fit in than it was about being attractive (that said, there's so much more to it – the search for identity, the distraction of calorie counting, the euphoria of hitting targets, the numbness of starving). In relation to anorexia and body image, for me it wasn't about being sexy; it was about being accepted. Anorexia had become my subliminal comfort blanket; if you took that away, I'd be exposed and naked. I'd stand out when all I wanted was to fade into the crowd.*

---

*   I realise I just said the opposite on the previous page – I was very muddled...

All this fuelled my anorexia. It bubbled away under the surface like some under-the-surface-bubbly thing. It wasn't dramatic, it wasn't exciting, it wasn't enough to notice – it was just part of 'my mental furniture'. It was one of those little foibles we all have, like people who finish every sentence with the phrase 'ya know wha' I mean?' Perhaps every now and then I'd realise I was obsessing about calories, exercise and weight more than other people, but I'm an obsessive guy – I do a lot of things more than most people (that's not a euphemism). It was more of a hobby than a problem. That's until something changed.

On 4 December 2007 I got a call. In fact, I got 11. I'd been in the kitchen minding my own business when Becky came in. 'Whose phone has an annoying jazzy ringtone?'

I knew exactly who had a phone with an annoying jazzy ringtone, but I quite liked the whole 'pub quiz' vibe she'd got going on. So after a couple of rounds of 'Guess the Ringtone' I fessed up.

'Well, your phone's been ringing non-stop for the past hour.'

She was right. I knew it was bad before I called back. No one ever rings 11 times to tell you they just got a new haircut. It was serious and somehow I knew it.

It was my sister. 'Dad's ill. He's been rushed to hospital. They think he's had a heart attack.' After that, I didn't hear any more. It was serious and I knew it.

Dad had already had a scrape like this once before.

When I was eight, he'd had a pretty big heart attack. Unfortunately, heart attacks aren't like driving tests: they don't get better the second time round. In fact, they get worse. Much worse.

I got the train home and Mum picked me up at the station. We went straight to the hospital. My sister was already there with Dad who was propped up in bed. There were hundreds of wires sticking out of various bits of his body – if he'd have been a plug socket, he'd have been a fire risk. He looked frail. My dad isn't a frail person; he's a big friendly personality who fills the room (and I don't mean that in a fat-shaming way). He's a warm, jolly bloke who likes to make everything OK. But everything wasn't OK.

Normally in cardiac units, they like to get rid of people: beds in the NHS are like quinoa burgers at Glastonbury Festival – in high demand. But Dad's stats were not good so they wanted to keep him in a couple of days. A couple of days dragged on and on. We saw people come and go on the ward, but Dad stayed there, in the same bed, the same place, not going anywhere.

One morning, while we were trying to burn up time before visiting hours, we got a call from the hospital. They told us to get there as soon as possible. Now, my medical knowledge comes mainly from binge-watching old episodes of *Scrubs* and the odd clip from *Casualty*, so I didn't really know what was going on, but I knew it wasn't good. I very much doubted that the cardiac consultant had a particularly tricky Sudoku he wanted urgent help with.

Mum told us how they can't give bad news over the phone, so we prepared for the worst.

We arrived at the hospital to find Dad in an operating theatre. He was getting an emergency pacemaker. The only time I'd ever heard of a pacemaker was during the London Marathon, so I was a bit confused about why he chose now to start training, especially just after a heart attack. The doctors explained that it's a little device that uses electrical pulses to make the heart beat. They said he was in heartblock – this is where the heart beats too few times per minute to sustain life. It's kind of like the heart going on strike, and, as it's a pretty important organ, that's kind of a big deal. All we could do was wait. We're not a very patient family (I've always been surprised that my sister and I were born on time, as I'd always assumed Mum would have got fidgety halfway through the pregnancy and popped us out prematurely). But there was nothing we could do. We were powerless, helpless and restless. We sat drinking vending-machine coffee wondering if Dad was dying in the room next to us.

After what felt like hours, we were told the operation was over and we could see him. He was heavily medicated. I'd never really expected to see my dad smacked off his tits. It was a bit like seeing Elmo smoking a fat Cuban while repeatedly shotting whisky chasers in a New York dive bar: it was out of character and a bit disturbing. Everyone was dazed from the experience. Being honest, I can't remember too much of that afternoon. Doctors were constantly popping in and out, wearing grave expressions and chucking numbers at us, which were apparently meant to mean something. For me, it was like watching a depressed bingo caller appearing and disappearing from behind that curtain. My mum's a nurse, though, so she knew what was going on and tried to explain. However, it wasn't great news, and any time she tried to explain, it just meant more tears. We stayed by his bedside all day. We would've stayed all night if one of the nurses hadn't told us it'd be better to leave Dad to get some rest. My mum and sister got up and left. As I followed them, Dad grabbed my arm and pulled me back. I turned round, and he looked at me all pale and weak.

'You're the man of the house now. Look after them,' he said, nodding to Mum and my sister walking out the door.

FUCK ME! Shit just got real!

Now, if this was a film, I'd have said something cool, or if it was a play, I'd have said something profound and intelligent. But this wasn't a film or a play – it was just a crappy Tuesday afternoon in an overcrowded ward, with my dad smacked off his tits on morphine. I didn't say anything profound or intelligent; I just made a sound as if I'd just accidently swallowed a fly and nodded. Shizz had just got real. Very real. How the frig was I going to be the man of the house? The only thing that I'd ever looked after was a shared sink, and even then I'd failed my room inspection because I couldn't do that properly. I'll be honest: I didn't really know what was going on. All I knew was that it wasn't good.

I've skimmed a lot of the details here because it's my dad's story, not mine to tell. One thing I will admit is that I didn't cope well. Different people cope with stuff in different ways. But I didn't know how to deal with it. Suddenly, everything had been turned upside down. Less than a year ago I'd been happily living at home with my girlfriend, mates and our happy family. Now I was living in a prison cell on the South Coast in a flat where we played Bin Jenga and my dad was seemingly dying. I felt rootless, dislocated and unsteady – everything was so out of my control that I didn't know how to cope. There was nothing tangible I could grab on to in order to make Dad get better.

So, yet again, restriction crept back into my routine. For a long time I didn't think my anorexia was about control. A one-word explanation makes the whole thing seem trivial – like explaining disability as 'laziness'. However, there is a reluctant element of truth to it. My restriction was the only area of my life that I was on top of. Things felt too... big! I was dwarfed by everything. Starving myself also starved that anxiety. It made me numb and that made me able to cope – being dull to everything made things easier to handle. When things were out of my hands, having something I was managing was amazing. And it really helped when I was 'winning' at it (when I was able to go longer without eating, when I was losing weight and exercising). When I could refuse food, feel my hunger and rise above it, the feeling was unbelievably powerful and it helped me get a grip. There was nothing I could do to make Dad get better (medically, I was about as much use to him as tits on a snake) and that made me feel powerless. However, restriction gave me some power back.

But when I was 'losing' at it (when I was putting on weight, unable to restrict and not exercising), that made me feel even worse – like I was on top of absolutely nothing. It made me want to improve, get better, push myself further to prove to myself that I could. That's what maintained my anorexia – the thought that I had to keep it up or otherwise everything would crumble. It's similar to descriptions I've heard of alcoholism and substance abuse; when things are too much, you go soothe yourself with booze/chemicals, but when you sober up and face the hangover/come down, everything seems worse and you need to drink/use to deal with things again. So, it's a vicious circle.

But Mum was concerned about my eating. That added a layer of guilt to everything. She already had enough to worry about and I felt selfish. I wished that there was something I could do to get rid of this, but it was the only way I knew of coping, I had nothing else to fall back on. If I got rid of the calorie counting, the exercising, the weighing, I'd have nothing. At that point anorexia was one of the few things that was in my hands and helped me deal with the situation – it numbed me, it distracted me, it soothed me. I began getting angry at myself for not being able to cope, for adding worry on to Mum and for being so selfish. Internalised anger didn't help, though; it only served to make me feel that l didn't deserve to eat, which created a vicious circle of conflicting emotions.

Not eating

I don't deserve to eat

Mum realising

Anger

Guilt

I feel selfish

So, it was all a bit of a mess really. When written down, this all sounds proper *clean* and thought out. But the truth is, it wasn't. It was all muddled. I didn't really know what was going on, what I was doing or why, really. More than anything, I just wanted to cope. I thought restricting, exercising and weighing would help me to do that, so I didn't really see it as a problem. Avoiding food was one thing I could be on top of and one of the few things that helped make sense of everything else.

Sorry, that got really heavy, didn't it? Here's a picture of a bear wearing a funny hat to lighten the mood.

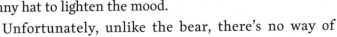

Unfortunately, unlike the bear, there's no way of

dressing it up: that December was proper shit. Hospitals are depressing at the best of times, but especially at Christmas. The staff tried to make the place look Christmassy by putting up donated decorations, but somehow that made it worse. It's like putting a crying girl in a cocktail dress – it jazzes things up, but it's still bleak. As you might expect, our Christmas got put on hold...until something amazing happened.

On Christmas Eve we got a call. Dad was stable enough to go home for a couple of days. It was amazing news. Sure, we knew he was going to have a quadruple bypass – a huge and risky operation – but this was the first bit of good news we'd had in months. We just wanted to make the most of our Christmas and put everything on hold.

OK, I'll fess up. My anorexic tendencies weren't the *only* way I'd been distracting myself. I had an idea for a book – a comedy about a teenage boy dying of cancer (a plot line ripe for comedy, right?!). The premise of the book was that this boy takes his imminent death (don't forget, this was still meant to be a comedy) as inspiration to make him do all the things he'd wanted to do before he died. In trying to tick everything off his bucket list, other characters end up achieving their own life goals and then it ends happily... just before the boy dies (it's obvious why it didn't really get much further than the 'thought' stage!).

The whole concept got me thinking about things people want to achieve before they die. It's something that really interests me. I began researching it and got strangely absorbed. During the process I idly ended up writing my own bucket list. Perhaps it was because Dad had faced his own mortality that it made me think of mine. The previous 12 months had been shit – I'd broken up with Lizzie, left the perfect life to move to a lonely, intimidating boozefest all before Dad had nearly died! I think it's fair to say it'd been a rough year. It was coming to an end, and it didn't sound like a bad idea to see if I could do all the things I wanted to do before I died. I gave myself 12 months to do it. I called it the 2008 challenge. On my list was...

2008 CHALLENGES

1. Become a Connoisseur of Something
2. Get Something Printed in a National Publication
3. Learn a Language
4. Get a Girlfriend
5. See All Different Types of Live Music
6. Overcome a Fear
7. Have My Fifteen Minutes of Fame
8. Go on an Adventure
9. Leave a Legacy
10. Do Stand-up

It seemed fun. It seemed exciting. It seemed like something to look forward to (which I think we'll both agree, following on from the past couple of pages, is much bloody needed at this point!). So, Christmas came and went. New Year came and went. Everything just kind of carried on. The weirdest thing about all of this is that the drama of Dad getting ill was not matched by any concrete resolution of him getting better. I don't know what I expected – doctors doing a synchronised dance holding placards which spelt out 'Happy Heart Health' (in fairness, that would've been awesome!). That didn't happen though. Over the months, he had to have tests, check-ups and appointments, and gradually all the signs pointed in the right direction. His quadruple heart bypass whittled down to a double heart bypass and then no bypass at all. It sounds weird now I think about it, but things with Dad just seemed to sort themselves out. It turned out that his heartblock had been caused by a cock-up with his tablets. He'd been taking dangerous levels of some drug which should've stopped years ago, but the doctor hadn't taken it off his notes. Over the years of usage, his heart had sort of got pissed off and gave us a wake-up call. I suppose it's kind of like if you have too much salt in your diet – on a day-to-day basis it won't seem to affect anything, but over the years that build-up will probably have some dramatic consequences which will only be remedied by eventually weaning yourself off it (I guess this is how it works...I don't really know!).

As for me, soon it was time to go back to uni and start all over. When things had been shit, I'd considered not going back to uni, dropping out and taking time to think about what I was doing. However, everything sort of carried on without me realising. So, I went back to uni but I had a different outlook (I guess your dad nearly dying will do that to you). Everything got put into perspective. I knew things hadn't been right before all the Dad stuff had happened; my mood was erratic, I hadn't been eating and it just felt like I wasn't really coping. It wasn't anything dramatic; I'd just been consistently under par, only just able to keep my head above water. It was like I was functioning at 60%, as if everything was sepia. Dad's 'heart fart' made me realise I needed to do something about it. I found the University Enabling Services – basically talking therapies like counselling, therapy and mental health support – and one day, after lectures, I went there and booked an appointment. They said there was a bit of a waiting list, but as soon as there was space they'd give me a call.

After that I carried on with my life. I decided to put more effort into making my little uni prison-room feel homely. I personalised my cell – bought picture frames, put up photos, posters, ticket stubs and a pot plant (which I killed in three days) and generally pimped my room.

Next, I decided to get to know my corridor mates, so it felt more like a home rather than Pontins. I spent more time in the kitchen getting to know people, chatting and having a laugh. They turned out to be pretty cool people.

In fact, we got on so well that nine of us agreed to sign the lease on a flat the following year. Then I decided to get to know people on my course. They turned out to be great, and a good little group of us began to hang out regularly outside of lectures. For example, one of the guys had told us about a comedy club he and his housemates used to go to. I'd never been to a comedy club before and it sounded like good fun.

I instantly became hooked. I never used to like going out to loud clubs where you couldn't talk to people and had to dance as if you enjoyed the music. However, at the comedy club you could get a pint, chat, catch up with people in the breaks and then have a bloody good laugh once the show started. Plus, the place we went had Russell Howard, Chris Addison and Michael McIntrye all before they were famous. But it wasn't their fame that got me; it was the ability to cope. All the comics were making light of the darkest of topics – being lonely, poor, single, ostracised and disillusioned – but laughter made it manageable. Humour was their way of making everything OK. If you could laugh at something (or about something), it instantly became less intimidating. The comics didn't get overwhelmed by things; they laughed at them. That was enviable – like a fun club where nothing was too much to handle. I wanted a slice of that!

As luck would have it, giving stand-up a go was one of the 2008 challenges (it's not as impressive as it sounds – when you're sharing a kitchen with 22 people, most mealtimes had a decent-sized audience anyway). I signed up to try stand-up for the first time at an open-mic night in our campus bar. I brought all my housemates along and that was enough for a good-sized crowd. I remember being terrified – I'd never really done anything like this before. Telling anecdotes while doing the washing-up was one thing, but doing that with an actual stage, mic and lights was something different. Luckily, the guy who booked the acts put me on last. I say luckily because he'd booked a shit-tonne of acts. It was gone 11 before I was on stage, and having been there since seven I wasn't nervous any more, just friggin' tired. That kind of helped. I burnt up all my nervous energy and now I just wanted it to be over. People mistook my fatigue for confidence and thought I was a lot more relaxed than I was. The bloke who booked the night said he enjoyed it. He told me they were having another comedy night the next week with Kerry Godliman doing a preview of her new show, and did I fancy coming down to be her support act?* I couldn't bloody believe it – my second gig and I was supporting someone off of the tellybox. I knew this was something I wanted to get into.

I joined the university Comedy Soc, Googled local open-mic nights and tried to wheedle my way into the local stand-up scene. As I got into it more and more, there were so many things I loved about stand-up.

---

* Important Point: even though he booked me as her 'support act', I was actually just someone who went on before her. It sounds pedantic, but actually there's a big bloody difference.

SOME OF THE THINGS I LOVE ABOUT STAND-UP

1. The people. The characters you meet on the circuit are amazing. I've met everyone from drag queens to ex-convicts and each has an incredible outlook and amazing story to tell.

2. The adventure. There's something exciting about being on the motorway at 2am telling funny stories and stopping off at service stations for a coffee (I LOVE service stations) and going on the arcade machines.

3. You're allowed to be different. When you're up on stage, you're meant to be different. Comics are clowns, from the outside looking in. As someone who never fitted in, that was bloody brilliant.

4. Making sense of things. They say comedy is just tragedy + time. I loved how people would look at things from different angles and see the funny in the tragic and use humour to make sense of things.

Comedy gave me a distraction, a coping mechanism and an identity. Everything began to simmer down, and as I became more distracted by the fun stuff, I became less worried about having it. The less and less I thought, 'These are the best days of my life', the more they became it. Things began to fit into place and I was able to get on top of my life and back to being myself. As my head began to clear,

I could get on with everything without being weighed down by all that gloopy anxiety. I was no longer overwhelmed by everything, but able to deal with stuff. That meant I didn't have to hide from everything any more, which meant the anorexia became less important.

Over time I stopped restricting as much. It wasn't an intentional decision, just something that kind of happened. Being me was OK. I didn't want to be numb from everything, because it was fun rather than overwhelming. As things had begun to settle into some sort of order, I didn't have to rely on calorie counting, weighing or exercising to help me. I measured my life by experiences rather than the numbers on a scale. Gradually, it fell further and further down my list of life priorities. Sure, I'd weigh myself every now and then, and I'd still have 'safe food', but I wouldn't be so strict. I'd certainly still be aware of what I was eating, but it wasn't taking over every waking thought. My life wasn't completely about calories, miles and ounces. I wasn't 'recovered', just less dependent.

Then, one day, I got a call from the University Enabling Services. A place had become available: did I still want to see a therapist? If I'm honest, I'd completely forgotten I was still on the waiting list. Suddenly, the thought of going to see a someone about that stuff seemed silly. I convinced myself I hadn't been depressed, that I'd just been through a rough patch and had been a bit down. I was embarrassed that I'd thought I needed proper help. I'd probably been making something out of nothing, taking it all too seriously.

Real depressed people don't just miraculously feel better over time do they?* I kindly told the woman on the other end of the phone that I'd been wrong and that I didn't need any therapy now.

Perhaps it was the right decision not to go to a therapist back then; maybe it wasn't. However, I should've learnt from it. I wish I'd taken note of the things that had pulled me out of my 'brain fug' and brought me back to myself again. They say madness is repeating the same thing over and over again and expecting different results. They also say that practice makes perfect. So, by that definition I was perfectly mad – not astute enough to realise a pattern was forming, but doing it over and over again like a proper numpty.

First year turned into second year and I moved in with nine incredible people that I'd lived with in halls. We had a blast and the second year whizzed by. Things carried on getting better and before I knew it another year had gone by. The summer holidays arrived and I headed back to the Midlands to Mum and Dad's. It was a Thursday and I was getting ready for a night out with the old school lot. Joe had called me out of the blue. No one had seen or heard from him, so it was odd for his number to pop up on my phone.

---

* In actual fact, they can. Depression, and most mental illnesses, can come and go with severity over time. So although it'd gone away for now, without facing up to it, it'd probably be back.

'Hey, mate, haven't heard from you in a while.'

'Yeah, I've been in Bolivia, Cambodia and Vietnam.' (This, for Joe, is not that unusual.) 'Anyway, do you fancy an adventure?'

Well, that was one of the 2008 challenges.

Twelve hours later, I was on a train speeding down to Somerset with my iPod, thoughts and massive hangover. I'd still gone out the night before, drunk too much and thoroughly regretted it. But I was also excited. What Joe had described sounded fun, which was enough for me. Best of all, I was about to fulfil another one of the challenges.

To explain what's going on here, I've got to explain something else. There are a load of summer camps that run up and down the UK, where people from abroad send their kids so they can improve their English. Joe had got a job at one. They'd had an email sent round because the site in Somerset had a teacher drop out. Joe knew I was learning Spanish (because it was one of the 2008 challenges) and was always on the lookout for an adventure, so he had recommended me. They accepted me and gave me the job on the spot.

I arrived at a tiny little station in the arse-end of nowhere. It was remote. *Really* remote. Even the wildlife looked lonely. It was the sort of place that hadn't changed in about 300 years (and that included the locals). Someone from the school came and picked me up in a van, we drove 30 or 40 minutes before getting to the school in Bruton. (Fun fact for you: there's actually a school in Bruton called

Sexey's School – two words that I don't think should ever go together!) When we arrived, it was lunch. I'd been up disgustingly early (having got in pretty late the night/morning before). I'd skipped breakfast in favour of the lie-in and hadn't eaten all day. But when I saw what was on offer, I quickly lost my appetite. The food was all pizza, pasta, chips. Everything was swimming in a pool of its own grease and even the salad was glazed in olive oil like it was just about to be fried. There were no healthy options, no calorie count and no choice. My relationship with food had got better, but it was still uneasy. There were 'forbidden' foods I still didn't let myself to eat. I still counted calories in most of what I ate, or at the very least had an awareness of my daily calorie intake, and I still weighed myself (just not every single day). Those anorexic traits never really went away. They stuck around like an old tattoo that people only saw if they knew where to look. But I definitely didn't really think of myself as anorexic at that point.

The school was 30 minutes from the nearest shop, and even then it only stocked newspapers, stamps and a strange sense that the world had moved on. The kitchens were closed in between meals and there was nothing to snack on. If you didn't eat, you went hungry. This was the first time I'd been completely out of control of my food – at home I'd cooked my own meals, and at uni I'd been able to eat as much or as little as I wanted, whenever I wanted – but now I had no control whatsoever. I would either eat at the three set times of day, or I wouldn't eat at all.

Now, you might be thinking, 'Well, you got free food, stop complaining.' But it really got to me. And I mean *reeeeeeeeeally* got to me. Food was all I could think about. It took over every waking thought. It even took over my unwoken thoughts (I genuinely began having nightmares about doughnuts, for fuck's sake). I began to obsess about how many calories might've been in lunch, how many there were going to be at dinner. I tried to restrict the amount I ate, which made me more hungry. The constant hunger would eventually get too much and, without thinking, I'd binge; I'd have three or four courses, eating rapidly, trying to get it all in before guilt would catch up. I was swallowing chunks of food without chewing. The teachers would notice me gobbling away like the Cookie Monster on a bender and didn't really know what to say. I made them uncomfortable. So I didn't want to eat in front of them – it was embarrassing for everyone involved. I began sneaking food into my bag so that my binges were at least private. But I got caught by Gerry, the chef, who told me we couldn't keep food in our rooms as it'd attract rats. The bigger the binge, the longer I'd starve. The longer I starved, the bigger the inevitable binge. It was a vicious circle and it got more and more dramatic.

If I couldn't continually restrict, I'd have to do more exercise. The teaching schedule was long – sometimes from 9am to 11pm – there was no time for leisurely walks in the countryside. So I set my alarm for the middle of the night to keep up my exercises. That didn't feel like enough, though. So I began going to my room in between lessons to do push-ups, sit-ups and squats to try to gain some control back. It felt as if I was bursting out of my body, like it was slowly inflating and bursting at the seams. Any time I passed a mirror, I'd stand side on, stare at my gut and pinch my paunch. Sometimes, when feeling really repulsed by myself, I'd punch myself as hard as I could in the gut, to punish myself for losing control so much. Slowly and undramatically, I began unravelling.

I was tempted to quit the job. But quitting a job because of the canteen is a bit like breaking up with someone because of their music taste. Plus, I needed the money. But the whole thing got to me more than I'd have imagined (and more than I even realised). I was too busy being choked by anxiety and self-hatred to realise what I was feeling was probably not normal. That was until something unexpected happened.

One afternoon we were on a day trip. A couple of teachers had gone for a coffee while the kids quietly murdered each other outside. In the back of a Costa, we chatted about anything and everything. Eventually, the conversation came round to the topic of the food. Everyone had a little gripe about the catering; it was normal to hear people talk about how much weight they were putting on. But this was different. We began talking about how the lack of control made us *feel* (and I know that sounds wanky, but I promise we weren't perched on scatter cushions sitting in the Lotus Position listening to Enya at the time). I joined in and began telling people about the exercising in my room, the calorie counting, the weighing, the stomach pinching, the coffee loading, the nightmares, the gut punching and the binges. I looked round and two of the teachers were looking at me like I was on day release. They began backing away, hastily made their excuses and ran out of the coffee shop, leaving their coffee cups spinning. However, one of the members of staff began listening to me intently. She narrowed her eyes and hung on my every word. Eventually, she said, 'I've been in therapy for bulimia three times. I still did all that stuff you were talking about though. Have you ever thought you might be anorexic?'

That was the first time someone *asked* me if I was anorexic. Up till then, people had either been shouting, 'YOU'RE ANOREXIC' or taking me aside and quietly accusing me of it. Being *asked* if I was anorexic rather than *told* put the power back in my hands. For the first time 'anorexic' felt like a term that might apply to me and, in an odd way, that was strangely relieving. If I could put a name to it, I could try to understand it. It was like discovering something I'd secretly known for years.

Now, you might be thinking, 'Why didn't you tell someone?' and the answer (to me, at least) is pretty bloody obvious. The reason I didn't tell anyone was that I didn't know what to say. I was still getting my head round it without trying to explain it to anyone else. Not only that, but trying to explain it to a *doctor*...are you shitting me?! If I wanted to sit uncomfortably in a chair for ten minutes answering difficult questions, I'd have gone on *Mastermind*. If I'd been pissing blood or sneezing from my eye sockets, I'd have gone to the doctor, because that stuff's easy to explain. At the very least it's something you can point at. But this wasn't. I hadn't got anything visibly wrong. I realised I'd got a problem, but I didn't know how to show someone when there was no scar, break or injury. It's like trying to explain colours to a blind person or show sounds to someone who's deaf.

Not only that, another reason I never 'just talked' was that I never felt anorexic enough. If I went around telling the world and his wife I might be anorexic, surely they'd take one look at me and laugh their tits off. I didn't have bones jutting out, I wasn't like a posterboy for Comic Relief or some new Tim Burton character. Plain and simple, I never looked 'painfully thin'. Now I know that doesn't matter, that anorexia is a disease of the mind not the body, that BMI is no more of an indicator of health than your shoe size is. But back then no one had explained it to me like that. Anorexia was something I'd heard about, but not really something I *knew* about. It was a term I'd heard bandied around the BBC – on *Panorama* and all of those serious, dull, sciencey programmes that 60-year-olds watch. There was nothing out there that related to me – it was all dull, boring and sciencey. All of this has taken time, hindsight and a lot of research to understand. At that point, I began to accept that I might be anorexic, but didn't see that as a problem.

TIPS TO HELP AT THIS STAGE

Writing a list of the things you want to do before you die

I know it sounds a bit morbid, but it's actually brilliant. If you want a hand, there are a couple of tricks to doing this one well.

- Be realistic. Chalking down 'Travel Back in Time and Meet Henry VIII' is probably going to end in disappointment.
- Be specific – so it's achievable.
- Be inventive. I always reckon dolphins must think humans are mental. It seems half the population want to get in a paddling pool and splash alongside bemused aquatic mammals. Use this as an opportunity to do something different, unique and specific to you.
- More than anything, be excited. This is your bucket list, your chance to do all those things you ever wanted. Enjoy it.

Giving booze a break

OK, this, far and away, would've been the hardest thing to do. I was a bit of a booze-hound. I always wanted a drink, I craved it. I knew it was high in calories, but I didn't really care – it was the one thing that helped and I would take the hit. It helped because booze is high in sugar. So my body was actually craving the sugar. Also, when you don't eat, your brain goes into anxiety mode and everything feels catastrophic. Alcohol helped numb that anxiety. So booze would give me energy and numb my anxiety...no wonder I loved it so much.

However, had I given booze a break, then it might have made things easier. I used to binge when I drank (I felt less anxious, so the consequences didn't feel as catastrophic). This set off a cycle of binging and purging. Had I not drunk, and invested those calories into food instead of drink, then I would have felt less anxious over a longer period. Plus, alcohol is a depressant. Over time it pulled my mood a little lower every day until I realised that I was clinically depressed...which really is no fun.

Interior decorating

When I got back to uni after Christmas the year Dad had nearly died, I made a promise to myself that I was gonna make my shabby room homely. I bought posters, picture frames, a pot plant...admittedly I failed my room inspection because of it (but I also think Sean's mouldy sink sponge didn't help either). Some people say that a messy room reflects a messy mind (which I find hard to believe, as I don't think doctors have ever found dirty laundry and unwashed plates in someone's mind) but I do think that having somewhere homely to chill out can give you a decent starting point.

Group meals

When we'd moved into our new uni flat, every Wednesday we would take it in turns to cook for everyone in the flat. Once a week I would be completely out of control of what I ate. It was a great way of pushing myself out of my comfort zone in a very controlled way. Being able to eat with other people also made it more fun, so I began to associate eating with fun rather than fear.

Get a job

When I was at uni I got a job as a tour guide taking prospective students and their parents around the university on open days. Not only did it help give me a bit more cash, but it also introduced me to a new group of lovely people, gave me a bit of structure and, on days when I was feeling shitty, made me get out of the house and be around people. Over time it was something that I really began to look forward to, and it looked good on my CV too. In short, it was an all-round winner.

Doodling

One of the things I used to love about lectures was that I could doodle while the lecturer was banging on. There's something so absorbing about drawing different pictures, focussing on that, which makes me forget everything else. Plus, I find it fun (and a little bit addictive). Don't get me wrong, I'm not Van Gogh (I have two ears, for instance) but it's just something that you can do in your spare time.

Vacuuming

OK, this might sound ridiculous, and maybe it is, but I wanted to suggest it. I don't deal well with mess. I'm such a stress-head that I can't cope with crap being everywhere. I always find that my mood picks up when I tidy the place. Now before you say, 'Oh, you can come and vacuum my place', I'm not offering my services. There's something so cathartic in cleaning things up and starting afresh. If my flat is a shit-heap, I feel like a shit-heap. Most of the time, building up the energy and desire to clean is actually much harder than the cleaning itself. Afterwards, I always feel much better and far more able to deal with things with a fresh perspective. Try it – the worst that's going to happen is your place is going to look all sparkly and tidy, and that's not such a bad thing, is it!?

Section 3

PREPARATION

SONGS FOR THIS SECTION

Florence + the Machine – Dog Days Are Over
Mumford & Sons – Winter Winds
Newton Faulkner – Dream Catch Me
Reverend and the Makers – Heavyweight Champion of the World
Coldplay – Viva La Vida
Empire of the Sun – We Are the People
Jamie T – Sticks 'n' Stones
The Clash – London Calling
Amateur Transplants – London Underground
Supergrass – Pumping on Your Stereo
The Cure – Boys Don't Cry
Röyksopp – Happy Up Here
Lady Gaga – Edge of Glory
MGMT – Kids
Rebecca Black – Friday
Nicki Minaj – Starships
Fun – We Are Young
Jessie J – Laserlight
Amy Winehouse – Valerie
We Are Scientists – After Hours
Hockey – Song Away
Belle and Sebastian – I'm a Cuckoo
The Buggles – Video Killed the Radio Star

This is where things get a little muddled. I want to be honest with you – you've made it this far (which is more than I expected – so well done, you!) and I don't want to stop that now. I don't really know what was going on here. I wasn't proper full-blown-shocking-style anorexic, but I wasn't 'recovered' either. It was something that kind of came and went – I focussed on the 'anorexic voice' different amounts at different times. It was like background music: the annoying fake jazzy crap they pump into lifts – it wasn't loud enough to cause a problem but still raised eyebrows every now and then. There was always an anorexic residue in my thinking, I didn't notice it day to day, but more and more it built up over time without me realising...like a credit card bill. It came in and out of focus without me realising and that's what makes this bit so hard to describe.

You see, I was much more comfortable around food than I had been in a while. I couldn't get rid of the knowledge I had about calories, but the significance I paid to them faded. There was still 'safe food', but every now and then I'd reintroduce something into my diet, gradually building up what I could have. I'd still weigh myself, but I wasn't completely dependent on it to validate me and feel worthwhile or a 'success' (plus it was only once a day, not four or five times like it had been). Sometimes I'd forget and this usually tended to be a sign things were going well.

Accepting that I had a fraught relationships with food was cathartic. Anorexia was something that I'd 'had' and accepting that was good enough. It was kind of like admitting you're not over someone – there's a helpful element, but it can also raise a lot more uncomfortable questions. Which is why I tended to keep it to myself. There was no point in making this bigger than it needed to be. It was in the past, I was getting on with my life and not going to waste any more time worrying about it.

'Preparation'

* Finding out what you need to do to change your behaviour
* Taking steps towards changing that behaviour

So I went back to university and had a healthier attitude towards food (and myself) than I'd had in a while. That conversation in Somerset helped me accept I might have *had* anorexia, but it wasn't something I was going to be doing anything about – I wasn't ill enough to need help.

The new term started and it was good to be back – university felt like home now. And when things felt secure, I didn't use calorie counting, exercising and weighing to anchor me down. Think of it like a job – when you're enjoying it, you don't look at recruitment sites (or at least not as much) because you don't need to. That's how my relationship with restriction was. Over time I began to drift away from the anorexic traits. It wasn't a dramatic change, just a gradual (and subliminal) shift in my lifestyle and diet. Things continued to get better and I began doing things that, at the time, I didn't realise were helping to keep me mentally healthy. For example, the 2008 challenges gave me numerous different hobbies. One that I got particularly into was comedy – seeing, writing and doing it. Comedy gave me an outlet. It gave me something else to think about other than calories, exercises and weights, and made me less two-dimensional. It gave me an excuse to find the funny, not take things too seriously and push myself. (I'm not saying stand-up's the cure for eating disorders, but I *am* saying that healthy distractions can be bloody useful... or at the very least a lot more fun – believe me, jokes are a lot bloody funnier than nutritional information!)

So things were pretty sweet when I got back to uni. I'd accepted that I might have possibly had anorexia, I was getting on with my life and was pretty chuffed with my lot. However, that had a 'best before' date. As soon as everything had sorted itself out, fate was going to shit on my breakfast once again. A big fat steaming turd-Daddy was being curled out on everything that'd taken so long to build. I was now entering the third and final year of uni. I hadn't got a friggin' clue what I was going to do with my life and I'd have to come up with something quick.

Luckily, Nick (as in Nick from Nick and Sarah in Section 1) told me he'd just got a chance to do an intercalation (basically another degree while still doing your degree) at Imperial College London. So, he was moving to London. I wanted to move to London. We decided to get a flat together...which was easier said than done.

I'd only been to London a handful of times and didn't know where was a decent, affordable place to live. I found out estate agents aren't that helpful if you ring 'em up and tell them that you want to live 'somewhere near the middle of that-there London'. So, that meant we had to keep going to London to scope out where was in our price range that wasn't too stabby. It meant we were spending a crap load on travel. In fact, the cost of living in London wasn't cheap either. Being two students, neither of us was rolling in cash and the cost of putting a deposit on a place in London was preeeeeeeeeeetty pricy.

Oh yeah, there's also the little question of what the frig I was going to do for work. I'd studied philosophy. It'd been a great course, but I was hardly what you'd call 'employable'. When was the last time you heard someone in a recruitment meeting say, 'We've got an accountant, we've got a lawyer, but have we got a philosopher?' Better still, this was slap bang in the middle of the financial crisis. Anytime you switched on a TV, opened a newspaper or listened to the radio, they were talking about the lack of jobs, rising unemployment and general doom. It was the worst crisis since the Great Depression (which I really don't think can have been *that* great). The media had kindly coined the phrase 'the lost generation' for the group of people who were leaving university...like me! If people with law, medical and engineering degrees couldn't find work, what chance did I have? I applied to as many recruiters as I could. They all wanted to meet in person, have a chat about my career prospects and test what skills I had. So, I was commuting to London three or four times a week for various house viewings, job interviews and meetings.

This was all on top of essays, revision and finals. They were hardly a walk in the park, either. Most of my modules required that I submit an essay as well as sitting an end-of-year exam. It turns out you learn a lot of stuff in three years. There was a lot to remember and even more to understand. Plus, they don't like making things easy in philosophy – it's not like science or maths: you don't get points for showing your working out.* So, on top of accommodation and employment fears, there was also the added anxiety that I might fail my entire degree after all. It all came at once, and there weren't enough hours in the day. I became so tightly wound you could have packaged me up and sold me off as a human alternative to bed springs.

Around this time, restricting, exercising and calorie counting slowly crept back into my routine without me realising. It happened gradually, unconsciously and with increasing importance. Thinking about it now, restriction was the only thing I was on top of when everything else was so unmanageable, and that made it kind of...comforting!? I was always anxious, always worrying away in the back of

---

*   I'm not saying that makes it any easier/harder than maths or science.

my mind – anytime I'd find myself having fun, the memory of housing, money and my bleak employment prospects brought me down to earth with a pretty shitty bump. I was constantly distracted by the things ticking along in the back of my mind. Having something I was on top of, that I could 'win' at and that was within my power was reassuring. I wasn't completely out of control, because I had one thing that I could manage.

Restriction also played a more active role. It helped numb my anxiety, self-doubt and fear about the future. It put a dampener on my worries and made everything feel a little less overwhelming. With everything being a bit intimidating, restriction helped make me a little more detached so I could deal with things. Some people drank their problems away; others turned to drugs. I turned to restriction – it wasn't a solution, but it was a way of getting by, and that was all I needed.

However, the problem was that it didn't only numb away my worries; it numbed everything. It'd numbed some of my anxiety, but it also numbed my enjoyment, enthusiasm and personality. I became zombie-like, indifferent to everything, just going through the motions. It was kind of like when you sleep on your arm – like that, but in your brain. I realised something was wrong and this time I decided to do something about it. Secretly, one day after a lecture on campus I headed to the University Enabling Services. I was going to finish what I'd started.

I was given humanistic therapy (that's basically a talking

therapy which focusses on the here-and-now, rather than trying to find a root cause – it aims to help the person help themself). It was good, but I spent all the time trying to describe how I felt and didn't once mention the anorexia. Why? Because I didn't know what was going on. I didn't have the vocab to explain anorexia. It's like trying to explain a creature no one's ever seen – you'll only ever give a gist of what it's like. I knew that things weren't right, but I didn't know how to explain that. One of the main symptoms of a lot of mental illnesses is impaired ability to communicate. Just take a minute to let that sink in: IMPAIRED ABILITY TO COMMUNICATE! That's medical speak for 'I haven't got a fucking clue what's going on!' So telling me to 'just talk about it' is a bit like giving a deaf person an audio tape. I wished I could 'just talk', but, you know what, I didn't have the tools to do that. I couldn't explain what was going on, and if I did, do you really think I'd need to see someone else to tell me what I already knew!?

So I found it tricky. Obviously, the therapist guided the conversation and over time we began to get somewhere. I only had eight weeks though and at the end of it I hardly left feeling 'cured'. I suppose it gave me a starting point, though.

Around that time Nick and I found a place in London that was in our price range and which wasn't a rat-ridden fleapit the size of a shoebox. We decided to take it. I used all my savings to put a deposit down for it – nearly £2000! Without a job, a rising overdraft and no job to go to, it was a stupid thing to do. But time was running out: my course was finishing in May, I had to be out of my Southampton flat by June and I had no other options. Getting a flat sorted something. Although it didn't solve all my problems, at least it kept some of the fear at bay.

Then I finished my exams. At least that was one more thing written off the list. However, it wasn't time to crack open the bubbly yet. Four days after my final exam, I moved to London. I wasn't really Dick Whittington – just a dick with no job, no money and very few prospects. I couldn't claim Job Seeker's Allowance as my course technically didn't finish for another two months (even though I'd sat my last exam four days before). I was up shit creek and never had a paddle. I went to interview after interview, doing four or five a day, haemorrhaging money on Tube tickets, pushing me further and further into my overdraft. In the evenings I applied for more and the whole process would repeat itself – let's just say it was hardly sunshine and lollypops. OK, I'd done my exams and found a place to live, but I didn't know what my results were and that flat came with a price tag. It wasn't like my anxieties ended; they just multiplied like a Worry Rollover!

With all this worry, restriction became a welcome preoccupation, a strange comfort that I needed again. It felt better to count calories, weights and steps rather than my mounting overdraft and rejection emails. I didn't think of it as something unhealthy – in fact, I didn't really think about it at all. My anorexia was a subliminal response to the shitty situation that was out of my control.

But don't worry, it's not all doom and gloom. I know this has all gone a bit *Oliver Twist*, but there's some light at the end of the tunnel (and it's not a train). Overnight, my luck changed. I had a recruiter who was block-booking interviews. She booked one that she said was 'an amazing opportunity' (however, if you've ever worked with recruiters, you'll know they tell you *every* interview is an amazing opportunity). It was at the publisher of *Marie Claire*, *NME* and *Country Life* magazine. It was a group interview in a big board room, overlooking St Paul's. There were four stages to the interview process and at every stage they told you who had got through and who was fired (OK, they didn't use the term 'fired', but there was a real *Apprentice* vibe going on). I could bore you for hours with stories of what happened in that interview, but all you really need to know is that somehow I got the job! It was insane! I couldn't believe it. God knows why they chose me; I distinctly remember using the word 'boob' during the interview and then laughing to myself. It must have been some sort of mistake – I'd be working at the leading magazine publisher in the UK, in an office that had a garden on the twelfth floor and an in-house cinema, and played host to people like Ewan McGregor, Emily Blunt and Daniel Craig while they shot various films (genuine fact). Surely people who work in offices like that don't use words like 'boob'. They use words like 'strategise', 'synergise' and 'top-down planning'. But for some reason they'd chosen me, and I was stoked.

It also meant that for the first time in a long time the stress was off – I didn't have to worry about exams, coursework, grades, jobs, flats or money. My luck had changed and I bloody loved it. Things had finally begun to get better and I was having fun! I always thought that I'd proper hate working in an office, but actually the people were a right laugh – we'd go to the pub on Friday lunchtimes, drink too much and come back drunk. It was great to have a 9–5 so that I could actually 'clock off' (which I never really felt you could do at uni). My work/life balance evened out and it was grand – we'd go out after work, end up going on a pub crawl and fall asleep on the last Tube home. Being me had just become bloody good fun and strangely stable.

At the same time I'd begun doing stand-up in London. In the capital around then it was a boom time for comedy – you couldn't walk past a pub, bar or club without there being a comedy night on. You know how they say you're never more than ten feet from a rat in London? Well, back then you were never more than ten feet from a comedy club. It was easy to gig seven nights a week if you wanted to, and I chucked myself into it. The more gigs I did, the more people I got to know and the more I felt part of 'the circuit'. In particular, there was a lovely group of people I'd got to know who were taking a show to the Edinburgh

Fringe. I'd always wanted to go to the Fringe, ever since I'd heard Dara Ó Briain talk about it on Radio 2 when I was 13. It sounded incredible and I was jealous they'd got the opportunity to go. However, they weren't telling me to rub it in; they were telling me to invite me along! They were doing a mixed-bill show (a couple of people doing ten minutes each) and needed a compère (a hosty guy). They'd seen me compère, said I'd done a good job and asked if I wanted to do their show. I couldn't bloody believe it: I was going to the Edinburgh Fringe.

Now, I just want to interrupt things for a minute here. I'm not saying this to try to make you jealous or spin some weak egotistical 'Dave Chawner Origin Story'. I was worried about doing this book – I didn't want it to be an autobiography, a chance to say 'look at me, see how great I am'. I'm doing this to try to explain my relationship with anorexia. So the reason for explaining all of this it to demonstrate that, at that point in time, being me was fun. When I was enjoying things, I didn't focus on anorexia so much because I didn't need to hide. In fact, I didn't want to hide – I was too busy living life to try to escape it. Calorie counting, exercising and restricting were all good ways of avoiding the dregs of life – anxiety, loneliness, failings, guilt. As that stuff got sidelined, so did my need for coping with it. That's why I dipped in and out of anorexic traits: it varied how much I needed it.

So, time for a graph:

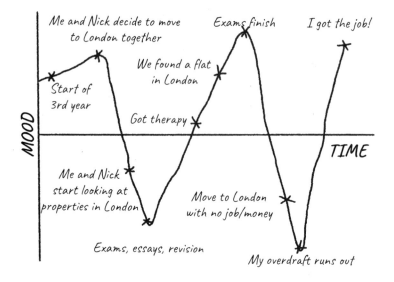

Me and Nick decide to move to London together

Exams finish

I got the job!

Start of 3rd year

We found a flat in London

Got therapy

MOOD

TIME

Me and Nick start looking at properties in London

Move to London with no job/money

Exams, essays, revision

My overdraft runs out

I was pretty chuffed with how things were again. So, I began reintroducing foods into my diet, stopped exercising as much and became more distanced from anorexia than I had been in a while. It didn't happen instantly, and I didn't even realise that I'd done it, but gradually my relationship with food became a bit more...*normal* (I don't really like that word, but I couldn't think of another one to put there). As I slowly and unconsciously moved further from anorexic thinking, something made me think about it again.

One day I was avoiding doing real work by hanging out in the production office. I liked the production team – they were straight-talking geezers who'd been doing this job longer than I'd been born. They kind of ruled the roost and had no problems speaking their minds. We'd be talking about one of those ridiculous diets in that week's

Woman's Own. One of the women began prodding my stomach and said, 'Someone could do with going on a diet, Mr Shirt-Stretch.'

Now, before you go thinking I'm going to blame anything on her, I'm not. Being honest, I should be strong enough to deal with people commenting on my appearance – the last thing I want is people being careful of their every word around me in case they might 'trigger'* me. I think that's more 'stigmatising'** than anything. I don't want people to wrap me up in cotton wool or change how they are around me. You can't change other people; you can only change yourself.

What's more, anorexia (a serious medical condition which has a higher mortality rate than any other mental illness, yada yada yada) doesn't come from being called 'Mr Shirt-Stretch'. Unfortunately, it isn't that easy. Most people don't like being told they've put on a bit of weight – that's not an eating disorder thing, it's a societal thing. We vilify weight. Think about it: if you tell a friend they've lost weight, they'll probably shake you by the hand; tell them they've put it on, they'll shake you by the throat!*** The word 'fat' is seen as an insult, whereas the word 'skinny' is seen as a compliment. Both are just descriptions and we decide whether they're considered 'good' or 'bad'. It's bollocks that

---

* A trigger is something that sets off a memory or psychological stress.
** And I hate using that word – it gets flung around the place so much that it's almost meaningless now.
*** As I mentioned in the 'Precontemplation' section. Wow there a lot of footnotes on this page...

fat is 'bad' and thin is 'good', but that's what we're subtly told over and over and over again (maybe through advertising, maybe through social media, maybe through the press, but I don't want to go pointing fingers because I don't think that's helpful). All I'm saying is that, socially, 'fat' is seen as 'bad'. So it's not an 'eating disorder thing' that I was embarrassed to be shown I'd put on weight; it's a societal one. (Also, Mr Shirt-Stretch – really!? It sounds like a particularly shit character from the Mr Men series that was scrapped very early on in the process.)

I looked down and she was right: I had put on a bit of weight. My shirt was a bit...'snug'. I'd been too busy enjoying everything to spend my days calorie counting, weighing and exercising. She hadn't pointed it out to humiliate me; she was just straight-talking. It was me who'd taken it negatively and I was embarrassed. I'd lost control over something I used to have a vice-like grip on. I'd taken my eye off the ball and felt ashamed, like I'd lost self-control of who I was. It sounds off, but I felt like I'd lost a little bit of my identity. I'd never been geeky, sporty or posh. I didn't have something to 'explain me'. Over time, anorexia had become my little hobby, my distraction and explanation. Being told that I was no longer on top of it made me feel like I'd lost something that used to help me make sense of myself. (I realise that all sounds a bit flowery and bollocks, so if it doesn't make sense, feel free to ignore it!)

It's important to point out, though, that that idle comment didn't make me turn back to the anorexia. Sure, it made me conscious of my weight and my body; perhaps it even made me think about my relationship with food – I dunno. But what I do know is that the turbulence of what happened meant that restriction crept back into my routine once again.

Everything suddenly sped up. A couple of days later I headed to the Edinburgh Fringe. I'd been nervous about it – I was a nobody, inexperienced and a Fringe virgin. However, as soon as I got up there, all that melted away. That first year was absolutely unbelievable. I could bore you for hours with stories about that first Edinburgh Fringe, but I know that's not what you're here for. Just believe me: it was fucking awesome. For some reason, the show got good-sized lovely audiences and made decent money. All the acts were incredible and since then they've all gone on to win awards, be signed by big agents and make TV shows. It was a genuine pleasure to do that show and I had a ball. Everything felt possible and I never wanted it to end. That's important because it made me do something very silly.

On the way back from the Fringe I considered my current situation. I loved my job, the people and the work, but I'd never set out to work on a magazine. For as long as I could remember, I'd always wanted to work in radio. I loved radio and would've given an arm, a leg and a left bollock to be a part of it. Still drunk on the excitement of the Fringe and punch-drunk on the feeling that anything was possible, I decided to look for a job in radio.

As luck would have it, I managed to land a job at a place which provided BBC and commercial radio with some of their interviews, competitions and content (what's more,

I didn't have to give an arm, a leg or a left bollock!). It was incredible. The first few months at that place were amazing and I couldn't believe my luck. I was going to launch parties in Leicester Square, spent the day in the studio with experts, politicians, celebrities (I even got to meet the man who is the voice of the Honey Monster, the Minions AND *Pokémon*). Admittedly, there were downsides – it was a ten-hour day, (and that was before travel and overtime), the staff turnover was high and the environment was ruthless. But you've got to take the rough with the smooth.

However, ever since I'd started, people had warned me about Ed, the owner. The stories they told were like something from a Roald Dahl book. Like the time he gave a written warning to someone for going to the doctors (a guy who later found out he had a life-threatening progressive virus), the time he'd smashed the coffee pot against the wall after an argument with someone who'd turned the heating on, or when he sent an email around the entire office telling people to stop flushing the toilet because it was costing too much. If you listened to all those stories, you'd think the bloke was the love-child of Donald Trump and Scrooge. But to me he was lovely. People told me that was just because I was hitting all the targets and over-performing, but I was sure people had just got it in for him – after all, everyone hates their boss, and this one seemed lovely.

One Saturday, as I was getting ready for a gig, I got a call. It was my sister. Gran had been ill, she'd been rushed to hospital and that afternoon she'd been pronounced dead. I'd always been really close to my gran and I was distraught.

We knew she was ill, but it was still a shock. I got the train straight home to be with the family. I asked for one day's compassionate leave to help clear out her house and help with the funeral plans. Ed told me I couldn't. He simply said, 'I'm sorry, but work doesn't do itself.' I begged and begged him. Eventually, he told me to take unpaid holiday and expected me to make up the time I'd lost in overtime.

When I turned up at work the next day, everyone was lovely – they'd bought me a card, coffee and asked how I was. As soon as Ed walked in, he told me to pull myself together and get on with work because 'this isn't *Loose Women*'. I had to take unpaid holiday to go to the funeral. While I was there, he called me five times. I told him I was burying my gran, to which he replied, 'I know that, but the world still keeps spinning.'

I began to realise everybody'd been right: Ed was a right dick! I'd moved from a job where I was comfortable, happy and content to Chairman Mao and his shit-pit. I couldn't tell Ed what a prize prick he was because I knew he'd fire me, I couldn't make anywhere else hire me; all I could do was send out as many applications as possible. I felt trapped. Everything was out of my hands and once again restriction, exercise and calorie counting crept back into my routine.

Then things changed. I managed to get lucky. Very lucky. I ended up at the UK's third-largest radio network. I was manager of the sponsorship and promotions for 118 local radio stations up and down the country. I was only 23 at the time and I was earning more than I thought I would when I was 50! It sounds good, doesn't it? Well, hang on a minute: that's not the end of the story. I was dealing with multi-million-pound contracts, managing people ten years older than me and was generally well out of my depth. I mean *really* out of my depth. One morning after a champagne lunch of lobster in Soho (genuinely!) I lost a contract worth £1,000,000. I was fired with immediate effect (which is kind of fair if you lose a million quid).

Now, I realise I've whizzed through all that, but you didn't come here to read my CV! What I'm trying to get across here is that everything was proper up and down. It was like...

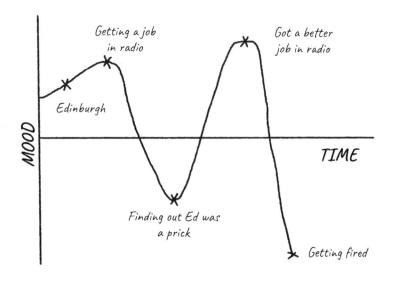

See what I mean? Alongside all this, restriction was one of the few consistent things I had. It was something I always went back to when I had nothing else to rely on. Restriction was something that'd help me take my mind off everything and, in a way, would make me feel better (even if it was only in the short term). It numbed me to all the fear, anxiety and stress, and became my hiding place when everything got too much. It's odd really when you think about it – that I found the eating disorder strangely comforting – but it was something that had never really gone away. It was a coping mechanism, and although it wasn't the best, it was the only one I had.

And although it seems really clear when written and edited, at the time it was just a spiderweb of messed-up mental shit. I didn't know I was doing this any more than you know you are breathing right now. It was just something I did: a process like your breathing.

Even if I'd have been aware of this, was I ready to give it up? No way! If someone told you to get rid of the one stable thing in your life, you'd tell them to bugger off. Plus, it wasn't *really* a problem, was it...?

TIPS TO HELP AT THIS STAGE

Hobbies
OK, this is a very trite one. Everyone knows hobbies help us to keep mentally regulated. However, I'm not talking about the usuals of 'reading, watching films and going for walks'. Make an adventure of finding what your hobby is.

The more inventive you can be, the better. Who knows, you could be an expert basket weaver, an unparalleled haiku writer, a gifted badger trainer. In the end, my hobby became my job and now I do stand-up for a living. Who knows, you could become the world's first ever professional badger trainer!

Flirting

At this point in time I took myself too seriously. In fact, I took everything too seriously. I was lonely, but every girl I met I was too scared to talk to for fear that she might be 'the one'. I'd try to chat to her, cock it up and that'd be my one shot at happiness gone up in flames (or so I thought). Obviously, life doesn't work like that. I was so scared of rejection, and so terrified of women thinking I wanted to have sex with them that I was never flirty. When I engaged in therapy, I had a long (and bloody funny) conversation with my therapist. I told her of my fear that women might think that I am a two-dimensional letch for speaking to attractive women. She pointed out that it wasn't debauched to try to speak to someone. So I began flirting and I loved it. I loved the cheeky, fun silliness of it and that made me enjoy being me more.

Routine

Around this time my mood was completely dictated by my situation: when things were good, I was good; when things were bad, I was rubbish. Of course, it's hard **not** to let events affect your attitude, but when things are so changeable, having some stability, routine and order can help you feel a bit more balanced. Even something as small as Tuesdays being movie night, or Wednesdays being a night where you socialise. Having something regular to look forward to can help keep you going when things are shit, and give you a bit of time out when things are going brilliantly.

Understanding illness
You don't have to be unhealthy to go to the gym, so why do you have to be unhealthy to go to a therapist? 'Health' isn't a fixed goal; it's something that changes and develops over time – so you have to, too. Sometimes things are great, sometimes things are shit – a bit of perspective on that can be helpful.

Role reversal
It's hard to tell how you're doing a lot of the time because you get too sucked into your own life to be able to understand what's going on. So think about how you speak to yourself. Would you let anyone talk to you like you talk to yourself? If you're constantly thinking you're a wanker, something might be a bit out of whack and you might want to start looking into doing something about that.

Section 4

RELAPSE

SONGS FOR THIS SECTION

Jess Glynne – Hold My Hand
Snow Patrol – Open Your Eyes
Amy Winehouse – Back to Black
Jack's Mannequin – Dark Blue
Jamie T – Zombie
Bastille – Pompeii
Of Monsters and Men – Little Talks
Rudimental – Waiting All Night
Icona Pop – I Love It
Blink 182 – Adam's Song
George Ezra – Listen to the Man
My Chemical Romance – I'm Not Okay (I Promise)
Jake Bugg – Two Fingers
Silverchair – Ana's Song
Pulp – Anorexic Beauty
Ben Folds – Still Fighting It
James – Sometimes
Ellie Goulding – Lights
Lana Del Ray – Summertime Sadness
Bon Iver – Re: Stacks
Dashboard Confessional – The End of an Anchor
Youth Group – Forever Young
Alexi Murdoch – Orange Sky

Now, I know it might sound a bit odd to 'relapse' before I'd actually got better. The truth is that I was swinging in and out of anorexic traits up until this point. I'd never been full-blown anorexic, and never wholly out of it either. This is the bit where I took a big nose-dive. Over time I'd begun to get more of an understanding of what was happening, but at this point I gave in and let the anorexia take over. By this time, I began to know I had a problem.

Being fired was strangely fun. Obviously, at the time it was proper nervy, but I tried to make the most of a bad situation. I set up a little comedy company with a mate, focussed on gigging and found other ways to make money. Accidentally, I found a job at a wicked tech

'Relapse'
* Return to some old patterns of thought
* Go back to old behaviours
* Out of control restricting/ binging and purging

company for a while. It was fab – we had a table tennis table, yoga balls to sit on and even a free beer tap. I really enjoyed my time there, but stand-up had begun to take off. I started getting more and more gigs, worked towards doing my very first solo show and even got offered a role as a panellist on a TV show – which nobody watched. (It was produced by the makers of *Loaded* magazine. I even did a show with Paul Chaplin – the bloke who owns the whole media company. He's a smoker so we did an entire episode where we both sat sucking pipes talking about books – it was great!) I was doing the Brighton Fringe at the time and getting in at 1am and up at 6am wasn't sustainable long-term. So I was forced to make a decision – office job or stand-up.

I gave in my notice and jumped into the unknown: being a full-time stand-up comic. It might sound all cool and that...but that's only to people who don't do it. I'm not having a go, and I definitely don't want to sound ungrateful, but people imagine you're playing to packed stadiums, going to VIP parties with Ant and Dec and getting driven around in a limo everywhere. Believe me, it isn't like that. Not at all. Not one bit.

This new lifestyle created worries I'd never had before. I was my own boss, and I found out that I hated my boss. There was no such thing as 'time off'. Evenings, weekends, even holidays were 'work days'. I was always working. There was always something I could be doing - writing, invoicing, booking gigs. When I was working, I wanted to be socialising, and when I was socialising, I felt I should be working. Basically, it built up a background angst that I was always missing out on something. That's not to mention money worries. Stand-up's hardly an easy way to earn the good bucks. I once worked it out and I was paid more (per hour) when I was doing a paper round than when I began comedy. One particularly slow week drove me to look into how much I'd get if I sold my kidney on eBay (the answer is: not enough). Regardless of how much was coming into my account, there'd always be money going out: bills, rent, expenses. And believe me, if you try to pay off your tax bill in 'knock-knock jokes', HMRC get pretty angry.

That's not to mention that I didn't really have anyone to talk to. Sure, I had friends and family, but there was no 'office banter'. It was bloody isolating working from home all on my own – just me and Alan the pot plant (who later died at 'the office Christmas party' when I tried to feed him gin). I got blacklisted from PPI sales calls as I talked to them for too long and weirded them out. The bloke at the local corner shop became suspicious when I started coming in twice a day trying to strike up conversations with him.

Then jealousy and self-doubt crept in. It felt as if everyone else on the circuit was doing much better than me. I'd see friends on TV, hear them on the radio, read about them in the papers. I'd compare this to my 'career', where I was usually playing to bemused locals in a pub. (The nearest I ever got to my name in lights was a gig where someone blu-tacked the line-up to the jukebox.) I felt like a failure and a laughing stock (and not even in a good way).

All in all, everything seemed a bit out of control. I didn't know how to open doors, push myself forward and progress in comedy. I didn't know what to do.

But my handy old pal anorexia was never too far away. It crept out of the shadows and back into the spotlight. If I couldn't do anything about my career, I could do something about my eating. It seemed obvious, if not conscious.

Everything about it was subtle. Long-forgotten routines and habits started up again. Slowly, it overtook everything and I began to 'relapse'.

(You might be wondering why I say 'relapse' with the little inverted comma thingies. The truth is anorexia wasn't really anything I'd 'got over'. Nor was it something that I was 'suffering from'. It was something that drifted in and out, a bit like a shit character in a sitcom. When I needed it, anorexia came back into the spotlight, but when there was no need for it, subtly and without my noticing, it would drift off. It wasn't as black and white as being 'well' and being 'ill'; there were lots of grey areas...which is probably why most people think it's a boring topic.)

Days became ruled by calories, exercise and weight. I began weighing myself in the morning. It was always before I'd eaten – I'd lock the bathroom door and force myself to go to the toilet. I wanted to be as 'empty' as possible to get the lowest feasible number. Then I'd take off all my clothes and tentatively step on the scales with my dangle out. I'd stare down (past my little Johnson) and look at the number on the scales. If I'd put on weight, no matter how little, I would instantly think of what I could do to lose it. If I'd got down to my target weight, I'd wonder if I could get any further and lose more. Nothing was ever enough;

I always wanted more. It was like chasing a rainbow, the goalposts constantly changing. I was always thinking about the next target.

By the time I'd finished weighing, I'd be famished. It was a gnawing, churning ball of hunger reassuring me I was 'empty'. This would lead to the second phase of the morning routine: porridge. I'd measure oats into a bowl. This might be done several times to guarantee I hadn't over-weighed it. I wanted as much as possible of my daily allowance but not a gram over the serving suggestion on the packet (because that told me how many calories were in each serving). I'd mix this with as much water as possible, to try to make it go as far as I could. I was left with a watery grey tepid liquid which was tasteless and disgusting. But that was kind of the point: I wanted it to be disgusting – if I could remove the enjoyment of food, I could release myself of the power it had over me. Whenever I enjoyed eating, I repulsed myself because I saw enjoyment of food as a lack of self-control.

I'd wash this all down with a big pot of coffee. I was always thirsty for some reason, so I was constantly drinking. On a normal morning I'd drink four or five cups of coffee; sometimes it'd be eight or nine. I always drank coffee without milk as it helped give me energy without the worry of any calories.

Calories ruled my life. Throughout the day I'd be trying to tot up 'my number'. I'd do this over and over again. I knew the calorific value of everything, but when something didn't have the nutritional info on it (like fruit or veg), I'd overestimate its calorific value just to be safe. I told myself that apples were 100 calories (when there's only about 60) and there were 150 in a banana (when there's only about 90). That was so that I had a little buffer to play with, just to be safe. Shopping lists became an A Level maths problem – adding up how many calories were in a basket. Food shopping was a nightmare – you know how they always say 'Don't go shopping when you're hungry'? Well, I was ALWAYS hungry. I became an expert on the lowest-calorie food. I'd go up and down the aisles checking labels, counting calories and hunting for low-fat foods. Like some depressing version of *Supermarket Sweep*, I'd spend hours deliberating which foods to buy. In the end, I'd always get the same things – apples, cracker breads and popcorn. They were my 'safe foods'.

'Safe foods' were things I allowed myself to eat. These were always things I'd eaten before, that were filling, without being calorific. The number of safe foods gradually reduced. I began banning more and more items, throwing away anything tempting. Then I stopped eating anything I hadn't prepared.

And that's the irony. I used to LOVE cooking. I know having an anorexic chef is a bit like a vegan who goes fox hunting, but the reality is, I was *always* thinking about food. I'd torment myself with cookery books, websites and recipes. I was always talking about food. Most of the day was spent planning meals I'd never eat. I'd have one meal a day and it was generally in the evening. It'd be something simple, with no carbs and a small portion size. I'd never use oil and would measure out everything so I knew the calorie count of the meal. That evening meal is something I'd obsess about all day, which meant I wanted everything to be perfect. So, while the food was cooking, I'd find my favourite knife and fork, get my special plate and make sure there was something for me to watch while I ate. Before every meal I'd go to the bathroom, drink a glass of water and switch my phone to airplane mode. I didn't want anyone, or anything, disturbing me. These food rituals gradually increased. Even though I knew how neurotic, obsessive and stupid they were, eating without them felt like the meal would be wasted.

Eating would always be followed by shame. I was a rubbish anorexic if I was eating, even if it was only once a day. I'd have to balance that out in any way I could. Some nights I'd be hunkered over the toilet trying to make myself sick, my eyes stinging with tears as I pushed my fingers further and further down my throat. Wrenching my jaw open, tilting my head, doing anything to make myself gag. Try as I might, I could never do it. It felt like hours I'd been at it, trying my best to make myself vomit, but only succeeding in painful dry retches. Thick, viscous drool oozed down my hand, my jaw was hot and aching, and my stomach strained from heaving, but still I hadn't been sick. My advice – don't make yourself sick after meals!

I needed to get rid of food any way I could, so I began taking laxatives. I took them in the morning so anything I ate because I was too weak-willed would flush straight through. It worked at first, leaving me feeling cleansed. However, over time I became suspicious that I was pooing less and less. Maybe my body was on to me? Maybe it knew what I was doing and was trying to make my sphincter reluctant to take part. So I began taking more and more laxatives. That meant my bowels became pretty violent. Believe me, it wasn't a good look – without warning, I'd need to get to a toilet urgently, and if I couldn't, there were *embarrassing* results. Like the time at a gig in South London when I nearly shat myself on stage. And people think anorexia is 'the sexy disease'! But seriously, don't abuse laxatives.

I became obsessed with ways to lose weight. I researched diet pills. I bought the strongest ones I could find. They had over 200% of the recommended daily allowance of caffeine in each tablet. There's a reason that taking them is a bad idea: they make you feel shit. I took two of them, which was 450% of my recommended allowance of caffeine for THE DAY taken in TWO PILLS! It made me light-headed, shaky and sweaty. One time when I'd taken some before going to a friend's house, I thought I was going to faint, my heart was going mental, I was sweating but cold at the same time. I think they thought I was just really into *The X Factor*, but when I started going pale, they found out what was going on (so don't go taking diet pills either).

These are not meant as tips, just things I hope you'll find helpful to consider.

* *If you're reading this and getting ideas, then you might not be 'in the best place'.*
* *If any of this sounds familiar, get help now.*
* *You might not think that you need it, but no one ever does.*
* *You will never feel anorexic enough to ask for help.*
* *You might not think your BMI is low enough, you might not starve yourself for days on end, you might know people who are worse than you, but this is not a contest.*
* *There's always going to be people more anorexic than you.*
* *If any of this is relatable, please look in the last section (page 188) for advice of where to go.*

Then I began smoking. Cigarettes are expensive, so I bought rollies. A pack of tobacco, papers and filters would last me a good while. The process of creating, rolling and smoking was kind of relaxing and helped stave off hunger. After I smoked, I always chewed gum. That also helped control hunger – chewing gum tricks your brain into thinking you're eating by giving you the action of eating without any of the calories (again, I'm not giving tips, and if you're thinking of doing this, please get some help).

As I've already mentioned, back then I was a bit a bit

of a booze-hound, too. I knew there were calories in booze, but the way I saw it, alcohol was like medicine. You see, I was a ball of anxiety at that point. When you don't eat, you become proper angsty. Think about it: whenever your stomach's grumbling and you're waiting for your food to cook, you're hardly in a state of sheer bliss. Apparently, it's something to do with low blood sugar and your body trying to get you to eat or something...I don't really know, I'm not a doctor person. However, the one thing I do know is that booze relaxed me. It was a way to take a break from everything – the worry, anxiety, loneliness and failure. It filled a function and proved very useful. The only problem was that over time the drinking got earlier and earlier. I wasn't really conscious of it because it happened over a while. Gradually, I didn't really think it was odd to have a gin for lunch. After all, it helped calm me down, refocussed me.

However, booze reduced my willpower. After a couple of drinks I'd come back and 'binge' on cracker breads. They were the only thing I'd allow myself to stock (apart from apples – but no one gets pissed and gets a craving for Granny Smiths). I'd smear them in BBQ sauce, and chuck them in my gob as quick as I could. I convinced myself I'd never eat again: this was it, I was going to make the most of it. The floodgates had opened; it was a race to eat as much as possible. Swallowing chunks of food, barely chewing, to get it inside me before regret set in. I'd be hunched over the kitchen sink eating frantically because I didn't want my housemate, or self-loathing, to catch up with me.

Each morning after, my stomach would be gurgling with a burning, ripping sensation. There'd be a tearing, bloated feeling - was I pregnant? Had my stomach ruptured? (I later found out that's not too far from the truth - when you don't eat for a long time, your stomach shrinks. The binging sent a big blob of food down into my belly which made it swell and stretch. The burning sensation was apparently the stomach acid burning away at those tiny tears...nice, isn't it?) So, to keep me distracted, I got up, got on the scales and the whole process started again.

At the time I didn't realise this was problematic. In fact, at the time I don't think I was really conscious of much. This was just my routine, and the whole point of a routine is that it's pretty mindless. For example, you don't really think about how to make your morning brew - you just do it. For me anorexia was the same: something mindless that I just got into the habit of doing. I was too close to my own life to have perspective on any of this. I didn't realise how much weight, size and food were always on my mind.

That's all the stuff I was doing to my body. You might be wondering what all this was doing to me - it's a good question and I'm glad you asked. As I ate less, my heartbeat dropped. The caffeine from the diet pills and coffee reduced my pulse further. My heart would get so low it'd skip a beat. Now, in all the love songs and movies that sounds romantic.

However, in reality it's bloody weird. Because it's skipped a beat, your heart makes the next one twice as strong to make up for it and sends an unnerving fluttery falling feeling throughout your whole ribcage. It feels like you've been hollowed out with a faulty whisk.

The combination of diet pills, laxatives and poor nutrition also made my skin flaky and dry. That sounds very vain and cosmetic, but it also had implications I hadn't really thought about. At night I'd be awake itching my shins raw like some flea-ridden mongrel. Sometimes I'd scratch so hard that I'd bleed all over the bed sheets, making my mattress look like something from *The Texas Chainsaw Massacre*. I was constantly knackered, yet it was increasingly hard to sleep. Over time it ground me down.

Memory was a problem as well. Gradually, it got worse and worse. The forgetfulness got more and more embarrassing. I couldn't focus on anything for more than a couple of minutes, constantly switching from one thing to another. Jobs got left unfinished – things I'd started, got distracted from and forgot to complete. It was like my mind was trying to run two programmes at the same time and began buffering. Conversations, events, sometimes even days at a time began to get forgotten. I'd start sentences and forget what I was saying. I'd walk into rooms and forget why. I'd have to say immediately what was on my mind for fear of forgetting it.

My mood swung more than a golf player having a seizure. I was impulsive and irrational. My default response was anger, annoyance, frustration. Becoming increasingly bitter, I'd sometimes surprise myself with how unpredictable I could be. That'd make me hate how much of an arse I was, sucking the fun out of almost anything. I'd constantly tell everyone how much weight I'd put on. They'd try to convince me I'd lost it. The more they said that, the more I was sure they were trying to deceive me. I was convinced I wasn't getting smaller, thinking it was my clothes getting bigger. After all, I hated my lumpy, doughy body. No matter how much weight I lost, it was never enough. I convinced myself that fat was the origin of all my unhappiness. Every time I passed a mirror, I'd smooth down my clothing and look at my profile. I'd push in the lump where my imaginary paunch was.

I began getting more and more reclusive and distracted. Over time I became more spaced out. I wasn't able to follow conversations. I didn't want to inflict myself on anybody else. Being honest, I always felt like a bit of a drip, the most boring, needy person at the party, and I was hardly fun to be around. Even I was embarrassed by my behaviour!

I was always cold too. It wasn't just a feeling of being a bit nippy and wanting to chuck on a woolly; it was a weird iciness from the inside out. The cold radiated from my bones as if my skeleton was made of ice. I had to take two showers a day just to keep warm. Throughout the day I'd have to run my hands and wrists under the warm tap to heat them up. On nights out I'd get so close to the outdoor heaters that on more than one occasion little wisps of hair set fire, and yet I was still shivering. We all found it funny – my flaming fringe as I stood in two jackets, a scarf and gloves, while everyone else was wearing T-shirts. The thing was, I didn't realise all this was related to the anorexia (when you don't give your body fuel, there's nothing to burn to stoke your body temperature).

Then there was the anxiety. I'd constantly be biting my nails, always feeling like I was missing out or I should be somewhere else. The lack of actual nutrition in my diet meant that my nails became brittle and starting chipping. Sometimes I'd rip part of a nail off, or bite so much that the skin at the edges of my fingers would bleed. The laxatives had washed most of the platelets out of my system so the blood didn't clot, meaning most of my clothes were blood-stained from my bloody nails, shins or itchy arms (combined with my *Texas Chainsaw Massacre* bed sheets, it led to some awkward conversations).

My kidneys began to hurt. Every now and then I'd get a dull throbbing pain in my lower back. Everyone kept on telling me to go get it checked out. I was worried it was the drinking, so I was a bit embarrassed, too. In the end I popped along to the GP. He ran some tests and all my behaviours had begun to take their toll. He said I had dangerously low levels of potassium. He asked what my diet was like. I shiftily said it could be better. He asked a lot of questions and found out I was taking a lot of laxatives. Like, A LOT. He said they'd messed up the electrolytes in my blood. My levels were proper fucked and he said it could trigger heart problems. When I casually told him that I regularly got heart palpitations, his little eyes popped out of his skull like a Looney Tunes character on crack. He said he hoped I didn't drink much as that'd put me at high risk. I told him I hadn't drunk that day...so far. He said it was 9am!

I was in danger so I got referred on. I had a bone scan which showed I had osteopenia. (Apparently, I had a skeleton equivalent to 'that of a menopausal woman'!)

My doctor actually said this.

Yet I never saw the anorexia as a problem. In fact, I saw it as my saviour, something that took the edge off life. I loved it and felt lucky I had what a lot of other people didn't: a coping mechanism. Without my realising, it'd become something to cling on to. I thought it helped keep me afloat.

I'm not glamorising eating disorders, I'm definitely *not* saying anorexia's a good thing – it made me a pathetic, twisted person and I see that now – but at the time it had a short-term benefit which lured me in. It was an obsession; the distraction, consistency and boost of anorexia was addictive. Like any addiction, it was greedy and took over. At the end of the day, it was all just a preoccupation, a promise things would get better. If I could focus on calories, exercise and weighing, I believed everything would sort itself out because it felt consistent. And consistency was what I wanted. It was a sort of anchor. Not only that, anorexia was the only other thing I had in my life outside of comedy. It was one of the few things I could use to measure if I was a 'success'. I wanted something to define me because I couldn't define myself. I didn't have a girlfriend or any love interest, and I thought all this would somehow lead me there. If I lost weight, I'd be more attractive. That'd lead me to 'the one' and then I'd live happily ever after. But as the years dragged on, that hope faded and anorexia took over and became my identity, escape, comfort blanket – my everything. That made me resigned to it. To die from the thing I loved was the ultimate achievement. No one could ever doubt that I had been anorexic if, ultimately, it took me.

And people did doubt my anorexia. That self-doubt got echoed the first year I did a solo show in Edinburgh. I'd been up there doing spots and sharing an hour with someone before that, but I'd never done an hour-long show before then. I was in one of the 'VIP bars' in Edinburgh called The Loft. It's one of those places people go to be seen. Well, it was my first Edinburgh doing a solo show and I felt like I had to do shit like that. I was talking to a reviewer who people think is very important because she used to be a judge for the Edinburgh Comedy Award, writes for one of the big newspapers and has been a judge on some telly programme. As we were chatting, she turned to me and said, 'You know what, Dave, I don't think you were anorexic. I think you're a white, middle-class male who just needs something to whine about.'

That hit me in the gut.

I stood there hearing the pulse beat in my face, my feet rooted to the spot. I was so shocked I didn't know what to say. I didn't have much time to think either. Suddenly, out of the blue, Al Murray came and gave her a huge bear hug and John Bishop came and bought her a glass of wine. I merged into the background and made a hasty exit, all dazed and embarrassed. She'd just said *everything* I'd been scared of.

It wasn't like I didn't know that this seemed like a pathetic, selfish disease. It wasn't like every day I doubted that I was actually anorexic – I still ate (even though it was very little), I couldn't make myself sick, I didn't have bones jutting out and my BMI wasn't shocking. It wasn't like I wanted to be like this. I hated myself for not being able to snap out of it. For me this wasn't about attention seeking; it was about hiding.

But I can't blame her for my 'relapse' and I don't want to be angry, bitter or hurt by her because it's easy to focus on the few people who said unhelpful things, but in general the comments, conversations and feedback were amazingly supportive. But I do think that conversation was about as much use as a trapdoor on a canoe. I spurred myself on to become more anorexic than ever before, to blend into the shadows and fade away.

As I restricted more and more, I became numb to everything. There were no highs or lows, just nothingness. I became a tourist in my own life, going through the motions. Someone once told me that 'the opposite of depression isn't happiness, it's energy'. That's how it was for me. Nothingness became my normality; I became apathetic to everything. I was completely oblivious to this at the time because it'd taken time for everything to become grey and pedestrian. I'd always assumed people with mental illness knew they weren't well, but on reflection that's ridiculous – my dad had diabetes for years before anyone realised, and no one expected him to know. Sometimes you're too close to your own life to gain perspective; it's like trying to make sense of a painting if you're only inches from it. My depression was something that had become routine and I didn't realise until something very out of the ordinary happened...

TIME FOR A QUICK STORY

One Saturday I'd been doing a gig in London. It was a sunny evening and the place felt alive; people were buzzing in the streets, laughing and making the most of one of those rare carefree summer evenings.

I wandered through Covent Garden, watching people glug bottles of Pinot Grigio outside packed bars. I didn't want to go home alone. So I pulled out my phone and texted a couple of mates to see if they were free. It turned out a couple of them were having a bit of a get-together. So I hopped on the Tube and headed down to Clapham.

When I got there, all three of them were topless in front of the telly, with ties knotted round their foreheads, playing *Rock Band* and eating Haribo. They all seemed very friendly. They're really good mates and have never been anything but friendly, but this was different. They kept asking if I wanted anything, if they could get me a beer, something to eat, a tie to wrap around my forehead. They kept hugging me, telling me what an amazing bloke I was. They'd always been nice, but this was on a different level. They were all doing this weird thing with their mouth as well, opening it like they were trying to eat a massive imaginary apple whole. I'd known these guys for five years and they'd never pretended to eat massive imaginary apples before (which I personally think is standard for most people). They were also drinking lots of water. It was all a bit strange. Then I saw baking powder and Rizlas on the table. It took me a while to realise it wasn't baking powder. 'It's MDMA, mate. I know you don't do any of that stuff, which is why we didn't tell you about it.'

I'd never been into drugs. I don't have anything against people taking them, but it was never really my cup of tea. I was always convinced I'd be 'that guy' who you read about in newspapers who has never touched anything illegal before and then one day has a sniff of something and pegs it. I always thought that if drugs were going to go wrong for anyone, it'd be me. But you also have to understand that things had become beige, grey and dull. I didn't really feel anything anymore – happiness, sadness, fear. So that fear had gone. I didn't feel afraid of dying, because I didn't really feel anything. What did I have to lose?

I took it.

I felt feelings I hadn't had in years. I felt happy. I felt carefree. I felt great. We drank, we smoked, we laughed. I had energy again, I had enjoyment again. It was like a little holiday from myself. That night I felt *free*.

DISCLAIMER ALERT!

I'm not condoning what I did (and I'm certainly not promoting it). I would never normally tell anyone this. I'm not the sort of person who goes around shouting their mouth off about drugs. The only reason I'm telling you this is that it's important. And it's important because it made me realise how depressed I'd been. I'd had nothing to compare my experience against until that point. I'd been depressed for so long that I'd forgotten what it was like to be carefree, to be relaxed and happy. Taking MDMA gave me a comparison and made me realise that things had not been right. But the problem is that I have a very addictive personality. I'd got a taste for it and I wanted more.

MDMA is like a firework in your mind – it burns up all the happy-making chemicals. They take a long time to regenerate. Generally, it takes at least six months. But I was impatient. One week after taking it the first time, I wanted to do it again. Then I did a third time the week after that. For that surge of emotion, the body has to pay somehow. That's why you get what are known as 'comedowns'. It's essentially an endorphin hangover. Your brain has burnt up so much energy giving you this high that it's burnt out afterwards. It's kind of like revving an engine for too long – it doesn't matter if you do it a bit, but if you do it for 12 hours, your car is probably not going to be too happy with you.

Having taken MDMA three weeks on the bounce, my brain was wiped. Nothing dramatic happened – I didn't end up in hospital or anything – but the morning after that last time I took it, I woke up unable to properly move, walk or talk. I had zero energy and everything felt a struggle. I'd overdone it and couldn't keep relying on MDMA to pull me out of this. Because, in between it all, I was waiting for something to kill or cure me. In the end, neither happened. Something I'd never expected changed everything...

One day I got a call out of the blue. Eating disorders were in the news and the BBC wanted to cover it. They needed someone to talk about their experience and had called me. I think one of the researchers had seen my show, or they'd got my number from one of the times I'd been a guest on local radio. I can't remember the exact ins and outs, but all I knew was that they called and wanted me to do an interview.

The next day I was at BBC Broadcasting House. I was met by the producer of BBC News, a small camera crew and a journalist. We did the interview in a little studio they had on site. It went well. A couple of hours later it went out on the one o'clock news. About half an hour after it'd gone out, the producer called me. She said they'd had a lot of positive feedback and wanted to use it again at six and ten o'clock. In fact, in the end they decided to make a feature of it on their website and host it online. There was a written-up interview and a link to the video.

BBC interview

People began seeing it and getting in touch. It had an impact I could never have imagined.

It all sounds very exciting and snazzy, but I was actually indifferent to it all. It's not like I'd been used to being splashed over the telly box. Even at the time I couldn't help realise how weird that was: that I felt nothing and was waiting for the excitement to catch up. In the end, I told myself

The interview also went on Sky

it was because I'd never set out to be on TV. My biggest goal in comedy wasn't to be on telly (the camera adds ten pounds – you could bugger off!). I've never aimed to be on *Live at the Apollo* or any of those shows. The one big goal I had was to host a night at The Comedy Store in London.

And a couple of weeks after the BBC appearance I got that chance.

Beat (the UK's eating disorder charity)* were hosting a night there. I'd worked closely with Beat as the show I'd done in Edinburgh was all about my anorexia. At first I'd got in touch to get a bit more information, to check that nothing I was doing was triggering. But they kindly asked me to be involved in some of the amazing work they were doing and I was only too pleased to help. Now they were hosting a night at The Comedy Store in London and they asked me to host it. It was a dream come true. I couldn't believe it. What could be better? Well, I'll tell you.

Two days before the big gig, I got a call from a mate. He's one of the stand-ins for *Mock the Week*. (Stand-ins are rehearsal guys. They're on set so the crew can check the mics, point the cameras and Dara Ó Briain can go through his bit.) He was booked to do the show the night after I was doing The Comedy Store but had to pull out. He was calling to see if I could replace him.

In the space of a week I'd been on BBC One, had the opportunity to do my dream gig and would be on set of my favourite TV show. There was no way I could ever have hoped, wished or dreamt any of this could be happening. All of these amazing opportunities just happened to land at my doorstep and I should've been blown away.

Now, I don't want to sound ungrateful. The fact that all

---

*   If you want any help, look them up in the final section.

of that stuff happened is proper brilliant and I was real lucky. But the problem was that I watched everything pass me by as if unconnected to it all. I didn't feel excited, happy or enthusiastic about any of it. I wanted to but I didn't. I tried to get all fizzy and pumped up, but I felt nothing. It was like being locked in an invisible vacuum – everything was suspended and mechanical. It was like living underwater – I was completely apathetic about everything, waiting for feelings to come but they never did.

The day of The Comedy Store, I remember walking around Leicester Square. We'd just done the soundcheck and had a bit of time before the doors were open. I was living in London, doing my dream job, about to do my dream gig! Tomorrow I was going to be on set of my favourite TV show, with my comedy God, Dara Ó Briain. Why wasn't I excited? Was I

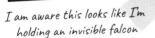

I am aware this looks like I'm holding an invisible falcon

ungrateful? Was I dead inside? I

told myself it was nerves. Eventually, the feelings would come...surely?

Standing backstage in the dressing room, I felt numb and a bit washed out. The music dimmed, the audience hushed. From the other side of the curtain I could hear the whoops. They were already excited. They were up for this, it was going to be great...this was going to be brilliant. I kept telling myself this, but I didn't feel it. I tried desperately to get myself pumped up. I started doing some shadow boxing to try to get in the mood (before stopping quickly, because I looked like a tit). Suddenly from the offstage mic, a booming voice echoed around the whole club.

'Ladies and gentlemen, please welcome to the stage your host and compère, Daaaaaaave Chawneeeeeer!'

There was cheering, whooping, clapping. I took a deep breath. This was it.

As soon as I walked on stage, the lights were blinding. A wall of light blocked out everything else out. All I could make out was the deafening sound of cheering. The fog from the smoke machine gave everything a hazy dreamlike quality. I walked to the microphone at centre stage and grasped it, taking it out of the stand. Still the audience was cheering.

Before I started comedy, I never thought about the performance from the comic's point of view. I'd always thought I'd love it standing there getting applause for doing nothing. The truth is, waiting for applause to die down is awkward (obviously, it's less awkward than waiting for the applause to come). It's an odd sensation, standing there in front of 400 people while they clap and shout at you and you haven't done anything yet. As I stood there awkwardly, looking like some clumsy human scarecrow, all I could think was 'This is what I've always wanted'. It should've been exciting, exhilarating, amazing...but, I felt nothing.

Two hours later, I was back in the dressing room. I was slumped in the peeling leather chair - it was all over. Katherine Ryan (who'd been headlining) had to head off to another gig. She gave me a big hug, grabbed her stuff and said her goodbyes. The stage door banged closed and I was left alone. I sat there dazed. The mirror was in front of me; all the lightbulbs surrounding it were glowing, lighting up the room. I leant forward and stared into the mirror. This is the part when all the emotions should set in. I sat staring, waiting; the excitement never came.

After I'd seen everyone at the bar, I had a drink and headed out into the night. Something wasn't right. I wandered round the West End with my hands deep in my pockets. I felt lonely but wanted to be alone. I felt bored but should've been excited. I felt angry without anything to be annoyed at. On top of all this, I felt pathetic for being so *delicate*. I was pushing people away: always too stressed to talk, too lonely to hang out, too confused to know what to say. Something wasn't right.

The next morning, I made an appointment with the doctor. I struggled to convince myself I was 'worthy' of seeing someone. I couldn't find a pattern to depression. It could hit at the most unexpected, unwanted times.

I couldn't walk into the surgery all smiles and happiness only to tell the GP I was depressed! They'd never take me seriously. I was feeling OK that morning. That made me want to cancel the appointment. But I resolved to see it through, even if it was going to be tough. I prepared what I was going to say, but I was embarrassed by it. Saying I was 'lonely and down' sounded a bit pathetic, as if I'd just come in for a hug! But even though I'd prepped, I still fucked it up.

'How are you?' asked the doctor.

'I'm great,' I said instinctively.

I flinched. 'Actually, I'm not great.'

Great, now it sounded like I had schizophrenia!

I took my time, carefully picking the words.

'Ooooooooookaaaaaaaay,' said the doctor, as I sat squirming and shifting in my chair. Maybe he thinks I've got IBS?! We stared at each other for a while. Half his shirt was sticking out, his hair was greasy and the bags under his eyes were like hammocks.

I explained everything – the lack of feeling, hollow numbness. He nodded, raising his eyebrows every now and then as if to say 'Tell me about it!'

'I feel emotionless, nothingness, indifferent to everything. It's like I'm just watching the world pass me by.'

'YES!' he shrieked, jolting slightly out of his chair.

He smoothed his stained tie against his chest and composed himself.

Which one of us needed help the most!?

'What I mean is, I understand what you mean.'

Should I ask if *he* was all right?

'I think it's best to put you on some antidepressants. We'll start on a low dosage at first. Come back and see me in six weeks and we can see how you're getting on.'

With that, he wearily smiled and gestured to the door. Would it be wrong to give him a hug? Where does a doctor go when he needs to see a doctor?

I shut the door behind me. For the first time I realised how difficult it must be for other people to hear about depression.

The light flickered in the dimly lit corridor. It reminded me of an old joke:

How many psychologists does it take to change a lightbulb?
None, the lightbulb won't change unless it wants to.

I chuckled to myself and made my way home.

TIPS TO HELP AT THIS STAGE

Getting help earlier

If a friend told me they'd got a lump on their chest, I'd never tell them to wait till it's the size of a melon before getting help. Yet I waited for a complication to become a problem. In the end, I just made more work for my future self. If you're worried about yourself, start doing something about it NOW. I mean **right now**. Put

this book down and go on to Beat's website (www.
beateatingdisorders.org.uk), speak to someone you can
trust or call the GP.

Talking to yourself

OK, this probably sounds weird, but a lot of the time I'm
not very conscious of my thoughts. Some people seem to
have a really clear, conscious thinking process. Mine is
more emotive – I'm more aware of feelings than actual
thoughts. The problem with that is that some moods
can feel really similar but be completely conflicting – for
example, anxiety and excitement feel very similar but are
very different things. So sometimes when I'm excited, I
get confused that I am anxious. Speaking my thoughts out
loud helps make me more aware of what I'm thinking and
that makes me able to deal with it. Admittedly, sometimes
it feels a bit ridiculous, which why I wear my phone
headphones a lot of the time – you can wander down the
street and people think you're talking to someone. It's our
little secret!

Believing I'm worthy of treatment

You can drown just as easily in a puddle as a lake. You
don't drown by falling, you drown by staying there.
Anorexia always wants more. I never felt 'anorexic enough'
for treatment. That's part of the disease – not being
good enough. The goalposts for accepting help kept moving
because I never felt worthy of treatment. It's something
that I regret. Learn from my mistakes.

Being honest with myself

I told myself I was in control. I thought I was enjoying all this. Aspects of anorexia were enjoyable, but that wore off as it took over. I got distracted by the numbers, activities and trying to improve. Other people realised I had a problem before I did. You might feel like you're on top of it, but be honest with yourself: are you really?

Realising I'd got depression

Emo bands do a good sales job for depression. It's not all artsy and poetic, though. Depression is shit. Truly and utterly, 100% turd-plated shit. Everyone's experience is different, because everyone's mind is different. Don't just take my word for it. See what other people have to say. Reading other people's experiences helped me describe my own. Writers have the ability to articulate what I've felt better than I ever could. Shared experiences can be vindicating, interesting and helpful. When I've shared thoughts with someone I've never met, it makes me realise I'm not alone.

Accepting it's OK not to have the answers

I used to think I always had to have the answers. I wanted to be perfect and in control. I wasn't. In fact, I wasn't even in control of myself. Some days I would be down without realising. Others I would be fine, but thought I shouldn't be. I don't really know how to work my laptop, let alone my brain. Accepting I'm still learning about this stuff has taken a whole load of pressure off.

It's also enabled me to understand how I deal with things judgment-free. That's made me deal with things much more efficiently.

Social media break

I have a huge fear of missing out. Everyone on Facebook seems to be having more fun than me. Everyone on Twitter seems to be more successful. Social media makes me think everyone's life is better than mine. That's because they're human comparison sites – snapshots of people's lives. Posts are invariably positive, exciting and proud experiences. That makes them pretty unfair things to measure yourself against. So, when I was so obsessed with what other people were doing, I wish I'd have spent more time thinking about what I was doing. Don't let other people's successes be your failure.

Relax

Taking time out is something I never used to do. I never found relaxing relaxing. I was too scared of missing out. If I'd have stood back from everything once in a while, I would've had more perspective. Getting perspective might've meant I would know something was wrong earlier on. Being aware something was wrong earlier would have meant the whole process would've been a lot easier.

Section 5

ACTION

SONGS FOR THIS SECTION

Jimmy Eat World – The Middle
Clean Bandit – Rather Be
Mark Ronson – Uptown Funk
Ed Sheeran – Castle on the Hill
The Lumineers – Ho Hey
Walk the Moon – Shut Up and Dance
Duke Dumont – I Got U
KT Tunstall – Suddenly I See
Elvis vs Junkie XL – A Little Less Conversation
Daft Punk – Get Lucky
Lost Frequencies – Are You with Me?
Vance Joy – Riptide
Amerie – Gotta Work
The Whitest Boy Alive – Courage
American Authors – Best Day of My Life
Frank Turner – Losing Days
Bon Iver – Skinny Love
Metronomy – The Look
Dustin Tebbutt – The Breach
Nirvana – Lithium
Itchy Poopzkid – Kings and Queens

I'm a procrastinator. As a kid, I didn't even have an Action Man because he sounded too proactive. I'll happily put *everything* off (which is why I'm currently writing this in the corner of a pub at 10.30pm with the deadline creeping up tomorrow).

So the action stage was definitely the hardest. It took a while to realise I had a problem and even longer to do something about it. This might be the stage you're at. If it is, don't forget, change doesn't happen all at once. Give yourself a break and take your time.

I'd been to the doctor. I'd been worried he wouldn't take me seriously, but he was understanding and nodded along as I'd sat there trying to explain what I felt (without really having the words to describe it). In the end, I think I started using my arms

'Action'
* A serious attempt to change
* Coming up with a plan, techniques and method of change
* You intend to keep moving forward with this change in action

and began flapping about like this was some weird game of charades. He'd prescribed me antidepressants and said that he was going to refer me to the eating disorder team.

Now, this might sound silly but I asked *not* to be referred to the eating disorder team. In fact, I refused treatment for the anorexia four times in total. I went to the GP to sort out the depression, *not* the anorexia. I was depressed, not ready to change. I didn't want to take the anorexia away – it was my coping mechanism, my identity, my distraction. Like an abusive relationship, it was something I knew was bad, but was too scared to leave. It beat me up, but it also protected me. I didn't want to take away the one thing I clung to, and relied upon when everything else was too much. Because, at the end of the day, anorexia had always been there for me.

I wish people'd told me what I stood to gain, rather than lose. I didn't realise the anorexia was actually holding me back and increasing my anxiety rather than dulling it. I didn't realise that calorie counting, exercising and weighing wasn't helping distract me but weighing me down (that was not meant to be a pun!). Everyone was talking about what I had to lose rather than what I had to gain...so no wonder I wasn't biting their arm off at the opportunity. No one talked about getting my life back; everyone talked about getting rid of the anorexia.

Sure, the GP tried to convince me this was serious. He said if I didn't to lose the eating disorder, I'd lose much more.

Newsflash – I knew that!

I'd done the reading and I knew where all this was going. And I know it's a difficult subject that makes people proper uncomfortable, but I'd begun doing everything I could to soften the blow – written the letters for my mum, dad and sister, begun making the video for my niece so she could see me when she grew up. I planned everything I could to make it as easy for everyone as possible when I was gone. I just wanted it to be painless and quick. Perhaps that's selfish, but in a way that's what all this was: a slow suicide attempt.

In the end, the doctor gave me the number for Lambeth Talking Therapies and told me to just chat to them. He promised they wouldn't make me do anything I didn't want to. So I thought I'd give it a shot.

I booked my phone assessment the next day. (That's what they call it: an 'assessment' – nothing to calm those nerves more than a surprise test. I got a calculator, compass and some scrap paper ready for the call, but I was relieved that there were no questions on geometry.) Instead, it was just a lot of questions about me. I talked a lot, bumbling and garbling my way through it, working on the premise that if you throw a lot of shit, some of it'll stick. We all know that if you get infinite typewriters and infinite monkeys, eventually they'll write the complete works of Shakespeare. I was doing the same with words – just hurling everything I had down the phone, in the hope some of it'd make sense. Having tried to explain myself once already to the GP, it was a little bit more polished (for example, there were no charades this time...but that's not for want of trying). I found it hard to try to explain what's going on in my brain-box. It was like trying to describe a colour no one's ever seen before. It was stuff I was aware of, but couldn't really explain. It wasn't as easy as just saying that 'I feel sad' because that wasn't true; my depression wasn't two-dimensional like that. It'd felt like I was numb to everything, kind of like a living zombie (without any of the benefits of being cool and interesting like zombies are). I was a shit, plain-clothes, entry-level zombie unable to get enjoyment out of anything. I was living my life just wandering round, going through the motions. I didn't even really enjoy the anorexia any more; the buzz I'd originally got from getting to that new low weight or the drive of being able to restrict for longer than ever before had worn off. I had to restrict more, go for longer and lose more weight in order to get the same buzz. But I'd reached a point where I couldn't push it any further. That made me feel guilty – I'd never been able to go for days on end without eating anything, meaning I felt like I wasn't 'proper' anorexic, which was part of the reason I was scared to get treatment for it – rejection.

Having spoken to loads of people about this, I've found out it's called 'Imposter Syndrome'. It's *very* common. Imposter Syndrome is where you don't feel 'ill enough' to deserve treatment. And I completely understand why some people might feel like that – it's not like you can really test to find out if someone is anorexic (which is odd, because they were happy enough to give me a phone assessment). Unfortunately, it's not as easy as going for an X-ray or CAT Scan, which is why I think so many people with mental illness take a while to admit it to themselves, let alone other people –they feel like a fraud. One of the things I loved about the restricting, exercising and weighing was that it was all dealing in numbers – black and white, right or wrong numbers. However, 'ill' and 'healthy' aren't that simple. I wasn't minutes from death or shocking to look at, I hadn't spent weeks on end in bed, self-harmed or spent hours on end crying. But I definitely wasn't well. I wasn't mortally ill, but I was definitely not well.

I spilled all of this out in one trickly, lumpy, garbled mess. That call was the verbal equivalent of a car boot sale – there was some really interesting stuff, but you had to trawl through some absolute shit to get to it. I explained all the stuff about wanting to get rid of the depression, but not wanting to move on from the anorexia. The woman on the phone couldn't understand it. I tried to explain, but I was a bit cack-handed at it. In fact, I think secretly I pissed her off. She got annoyed and said, 'Bottom line: we can try to get rid of the depression, but we won't be able to do anything unless we get rid of the anorexia.'

I'm always sceptical of people's retelling of dramatic 'turning points' – life isn't some clean-cut Disney movie like a lot of people try to make it out to be. However, if I had to pick one, that call would be it.

The woman explained that once you stop feeding your body, you also stop feeding your mind. Your brain can't work on empty; without any fuel, it can't do any of the fun stuff. It makes sense; you wouldn't expect your phone to work without any charge – it's the same for the brain. I'd never really thought about it like that before.

So I was faced with a choice: either I keep the depression as long as it takes the anorexia to reach its course or I get rid of the anorexia, get rid of everything I'd used to cope and hope the depression goes away. It was *Catch 22*, *Deal or No Deal* and *Mission: Impossible* all rolled into one. I asked for a bit of time to ponder it.

I was proper scared to get rid of the anorexia. I didn't know how it'd work, what I'd need to do and even the sort of person I'd be without it (which I know sounds wanky, but is honestly true). But, you know what, things were shit and I was ready for a new start. It was a fresh slate, a clean break, a blank canvas, an opportunity to rattle off ridiculous metaphors...again! So I called them up and said I'd like to be referred to the Eating Disorders Services.

I got referred to the Maudsley – the best Eating Disorder Unit in the world. It's the Hogwarts of Mental Health. The Eating Disorder Unit is on the campus of Anxiety & Trauma; therefore, there are a lot of anxious people walking around (obviously). Why, in God's name, then, did someone decide to stick it opposite A&E? Perhaps it's for exposure therapy – there are ambulances, police cars and sirens and even a fucking helipad on the roof! It's more like *CSI* than *Holby City*!

The whole campus is an illogical warren of multiple buildings. Trying to find where I was meant to be was like an episode of *The Crystal Maze* – in the end I had to ask a cleaner where I was going. He told me to go down the corridor, round the corner, climb through the secret door, pace ten steps from the fallen oak tree and solve a riddle to get through the guarded passage. It's hardly ideal for anxious people – a bit like opening an operating theatre in a landfill site. Best of all, when I got to the Eating Disorder Unit, I found out it's above a restaurant! It's like the whole place has never heard of the concept of irony. Either that or the architect built it as a bloody good laugh.

I had to go for an initial assessment (another test! I swear I've done more exams for my mental health than I did for my entire degree). I'd never been on an Eating Disorder Unit before so I didn't know what to expect. I'm not going to lie, I was a bit disappointed to find it was just a long corridor with rooms coming off it. Nothing dramatic or theatrical, just a regular corridor. Immediately on the left was a little cosy waiting room and a selection of magazines...including *Cat Monthly* (who could be scared of a place that subscribes to *Cat Monthly*?!). I was told it was just a chat and so I didn't need to prepare anything like a collage made out of pasta shells. I was met by a lovely woman called Dr Ulrike Schmidt (she's like the Professor McGonagall of Eating Disorders). We went through to a little room with nothing but two chairs, a table and a big box of tissues. I couldn't help but look at the multipack of Kleenex and think, 'I'm glad she thinks this is going to go well!'

My biggest worry going into that room was that she was going to say I wasn't anorexic. All the articles I'd found about anorexia were people much 'better' at it than me.

They'd all been minutes away from death, weighing less than a bag of crisps, fainting at every turn. I wasn't noticeably/shockingly skinny, I'd never gone weeks on end without food, I'd never snapped my arm trying to open a car door or got blown away by a strong gust of wind. I'll be honest: that sort of article hadn't really motivated me to get help much – it kind of inferred that other people were more anorexic than me, so I probably didn't deserve to be here. That's not to mention the stories I'd heard about people being rejected from treatment. There's so much stuff out there about people getting turned away for not being 'anorexic enough'. What I never really thought about, though, was that those stories are the only ones that get told because bad news sells. It's awful but it's true – when was the last time you watched *News at Ten* for a pick-me-up? Think about it: which one of these are you going to read:

(1) a story about a violent hooded gang going door-to-door rampaging through your neighbourhood armed with guns, machetes and meat cleavers

or:

(2) a story about a local gang of Cub Scouts going door-to-door selling cakes for a local Donkey Sanctuary armed with Battenberg, lemon drizzle and Vicky sponge?

Call me cynical, but I don't think even the Cub Scouts would read their story given that choice. Shocking stories are the ones that grab you and suck you in. It kind of makes sense when you think about it – the knife-wielding gang is a teensy bit more of a concern than Arkela and his cupcakes. It's called 'negativity bias', which isn't the new Morrissey album; it's a theory which states that stories of a negative nature have a greater impact than positive accounts. Basically, the more shocking a story, the more gripping it is. Now this is all well and good, but you might be thinking, 'Where are you going with this?' It's a good question and I'm glad you asked.

I wasn't *Daily-Mail*-shocking-style anorexic, I didn't look like a posterboy for Comic Relief and never had a rib cage which you could play like a xylophone. I never felt 'anorexic enough' to admit I had a problem. Negativity bias meant that all the stories I read, heard or watched were the most extreme cases. That made me feel like a fraud, like I wasn't really ill like people in newspapers or on TV. Let's also not forget that helpful reviewer in Edinburgh. So, as I got on to the Eating Disorder Unit to be assessed, all this rattled round my brain like an errant pinball in a faulty machine. I couldn't shake the feeling that I shouldn't be there, that I wasn't a 'proper' anorexic. I had Imposter Syndrome and I had it baaaaaaaaaaaaaaaaaaad.*

---

*   That's meant to be read with a sassy accent. Maybe a finger click or two if you really feel it.

Ulrike took me through to a little interview room. We sat down and stared at the Kleenex. I fessed up that I was worried she was going say I wasn't anorexic at all, that I was making it all up and should get a grip. However, she didn't say that. She said that other people's accounts are exactly that – other people's. Different people struggle in different ways. BMI, weights and waist sizes are all measures of the body, not the mind. It's not about numbers – you can drown in a puddle just as much as you can in a lake. Eating Disorders aren't about comparison, they're about impact. And I remember thinking, 'OK, you win this round, McGonagall, but you're not going to win that easily.'

The assessment went on for hours (probably longer than it should). I spilled my heart out, started from the beginning, told her about *Sparkleshark*, Lizzie, Dad's heart attack, teaching and everything in between. By now there was much more shape to the story and I could get to the point a little bit more (I'll put it this way: there were no charades). All the while she scribbled down notes on her pad of paper and I became increasingly curious what was on that page – maybe she was just doodling? Perhaps at the end she'd give me a caricature she'd drawn of me? She never once rushed me, despite my rambling like a guest on *Desert Island Discs*. Eventually, I ran out of things to say and felt completely exhausted, but it wasn't over yet.

One of the things they have to do to assess you for eating disorders is to weigh you. I don't think that's helpful – it feels almost like you've got to prove yourself. However, them's the rules and it was something I'd been told to expect. I was about as nervous as a long-tailed cat in a room full of rocking chairs. Despite it being late December, I'd worn a T-shirt and flannel trousers like someone who'd been hoping global warming was really going to catch on. But they were the lightest clothes I'd got – I had to prove to them I was ill; it was 'Anorexia: The Audition'.

We got into the little white room. There was nothing but a table and a weighing scale – it couldn't have been more ominous if they'd had a copy of the Last Rites blu-tacked to the wall. I asked if I could take my shoes off; she said it was OK. Then I asked if I could take off my top and she pursed her lips and shook her head. 'How about my trousers?' I said, sounding like a bloke desperate to get to third base. 'Just your shoes will be fine,' nodded Ulrike.

I was terrified about what my weight would be. Of course, I'd weighed myself that morning. In fact, I'd weighed myself three times that morning (pre-pee, post-pee and one for good luck). I know now that my anorexia wasn't really about weight; it was about all the stuff underlying that – the feeling of not being good enough and trying to get a grip. One of the things that appealed to me with the anorexia was the ability to measure something. Success and failure in most aspects of life are points of view, but exercising and calorie counting were numbers. There's stability in numbers, some way to measure 'success'. At the time I didn't have this insight, though – everything in my noggin was a bit of a mess.

Ulrike nodded, noted down the number and closed her pad. 'I'm going to have to go and consult some notes and get back to you. If you wouldn't mind making yourself comfortable in the waiting room, I will be with you shortly.' I wanted to make a joke about already being in 'The Weighting Room' but thought better of it. I nervously shuffled off to read *Cat Monthly*. Of course, I couldn't, though – not only because it is a magazine like *Playboy* and people only buy it for the pictures, but also because I was shitting bricks. Not literally, obviously (I've never eaten LEGO®). I was shaking with nerves. What if I wasn't anorexic? What if I was making this all up? What if McGonagall didn't believe me?

After what felt like an eternity she came back, thanked me for waiting and showed me through to her office (which, I was disappointed to see, didn't have any wands, broomsticks or caged owls). We sat down and I waited for the news. She looked serious. I remember the long pauses and feeling the tension building like *The X Factor* Finals. There might have been some lasers and dry ice in her office, or I might have imagined that with hindsight. Eventually, she looked up from her notes, narrowed her eyes and said slowly, 'I'm really sorry to tell you, Dave, but you're severely clinically anorexic. We're going to have to start treatment as soon as we can.'

Everything stopped. There was a jolt in my stomach.

'THANK YOU THANK YOU THANK YOU!'

I got up and hugged her. Her eyes shot out of her head and she stayed as stiff as a board.

I was elated. Someone believed me. *She* believed me. I wasn't making this stuff up, I wasn't just being a drama queen, I wasn't a fraud.

I'd been so nervous that they'd tell me to bugger off that I hadn't thought what it'd mean if I could start treatment. Having worried for so long about the worst possible outcome, I'd never even considered what the best would be. OK, I was scared about what 'recovery' might mean, how it'd work and who I'd be afterwards, but perhaps it might be easier, better, more fun? It was a fresh slate, a clean break, a blank canvas, an opportunity to rattle off ridiculous metaphors...for the final time.

Being taken seriously, being able to start treatment, meant that someone did believe me. It felt like a way out, like hope, a new beginning.

So I was given therapy. People who've never had therapy are always eager to hear what it's like. I think they're secretly wondering if you're made to lie down on one of those bed/ sofa things and talk about your father while analysing ink blots. Sorry to disappoint, but it isn't like that. Hollywood's version of therapy is wildly different to the NHS version – less dramatic, less exciting and *much* less budget.

I find it mental* that people would be reluctant to go

---

*   Forgive the unintentional pun.

to therapy. You get an hour a week to talk about nothing but yourself – what's not to love? I had psychotherapy. The whole aim of it was to help me become aware of hidden patterns in stuff I did which fed the anorexia.* My therapist was cracking – a lovely woman called Elaine, who was patient, understanding and bloody funny. She asked loads about personal relationships in order to make links between past and present actions. Think of it like *Cluedo* with behaviour patterns.

Therapy's a weird process. At first I found it frustrating – there was a lot of talk and not much action (which always made me wonder if the song 'A Little Less Conversation' is about therapy). I'm not the most patient person in the world. In fact, I might be *the least* patient person in the world (I don't know, I don't have the time to do the research). Unfortunately, therapy needs time, patience and commitment...all the boring stuff, basically. But it's worth it. Things I never thought would be relevant turned out to be crucial and things I thought might be a huge deal actually turned out to be nothing much. I discovered that the anorexia was one way of trying to cling to something, to distract me when everything else felt too 'big'. I found that I was drawn to the restriction, exercise and weighing because most of the time I felt like a failure. Calories, distances and kilos were things I could count and therefore I could track them. That's what kept it going for so long

*   ...and that one.

– when I was 'winning'* at it, anorexia was enjoyable – a stabiliser and an identity. It was something I could do, I could understand and I could be. But when I was 'losing' at it, restriction, exercise and weights seemed the only way to get back on top. Anorexia had become a way of helping understand and cope with everything in life – the good, bad and indifferent. It was a clear-cut way of measuring if I was succeeding at something and the promise that I'd feel worthwhile when I got there.

No wonder I hadn't wanted to give it up – anorexia distracted, stabilised and explained me. It also helped numb me to unwanted emotions and helped me become detached from everything.

I learnt this and so much more. It was tricky but brilliant. Yet, at the end of it all, I still wouldn't say therapy's a 'cure'. It's not like a course you on, get a certificate, badge and a qualification and then you can deal with anything life lobs at you. There's no black belt in therapy. It's not about 'curing' shit; it's about understanding different parts of your personality, increasing the good stuff and dialling down the stuff you struggle with (like a volume equaliser for your brain-bonce).

Although I don't think it's a cure, I don't think that makes it any less important – no one'll ever eradicate crime, but that doesn't mean you should grab a crow-bar and break into your local NatWest. If 'recovery' means anything,

---

*   Able to restrict, exercise and lose weight.

it's about helping you help yourself. And it's something you have to do for yourself. Other people can help guide, recognise and understand behaviours, but ultimately you have to do it for yourself. No one finishes any marathons by just reading blogs. When it comes to the graft (reaching recovery goals, changing behaviours and pushing yourself), you've got to do it for yourself.

It'd be wrong to pretend it was a smooth transition. 'Recovery' is a process, not a state. It's an ongoing improvement – you'll probably fuck up every now and then, but that's OK because we're all fuck-ups every now and then (me included...probably more than most). It might sound like some hippy-dippy bullcrap, but it isn't really. And you know what, it's fair enough when you think about it – if you go to a gym, you don't expect a personal trainer to hand you a ripped body you can just crawl inside and walk around in for ever. It takes work, effort and dedication – it's something that develops over time and needs to be monitored. Mental and physical health aren't too different – after all, the brain's just a muscle and it needs to be trained and kept in good shape, too.

I don't want to be all cutesy and twee about it either. There were some bits of 'recovery' I found bloody tough. For example, the weight gain. I frigging hated that. But you can't complain about it because most people will say it sounds like a chuffin' dream to have to *put on* weight. But it wasn't as easy as just grabbing a tub of Ben & Jerry's and getting stuck in. Why? Well, restricting, calorie counting and reducing my weight had defined me. I realise that might sound a little goofy, but the anorexia had been one of the only stable things I'd got. It'd been the one thing I'd used to try to make sense of everything – when everything was changing, anorexia was always running in the background. It was a coping mechanism – a diseased one, but the only one I had. It'd been a way of life for so long that I worried if I got rid of all that stuff, I'd lose control of everything.

That's not to mention the chemical changes in your brain as well. No one warned me about that. You see, like I said earlier, one of the things I enjoyed about the anorexia was that it numbed me. One of the many things it numbed was my masculinity. When your brain's busy starving, it stops releasing some of the chemicals it doesn't have energy to supply. Some of the first to go are the non-essential ones like testosterone (the 'manly' chemical). I didn't know this when I first became anorexic; it was an unexpected side effect I enjoyed. I'd never been a 'manly man'. At school I'd played rugby, but had never really been that good as I didn't really understand the whole aggression to it – a lot of my mates would get stuck in, hurl themselves at players and scrabble for the ball. I'd stand back from all the commotion shouting encouraging organisational commands such as 'If we just form an orderly queue, you can all have a go with the inflatable egg!' As I got less and less testosterone, I became more and more camp. I enjoyed being camp, because it made me less of a threat. And I'm probably going to have to explain that as well, aren't I?

Basically, I always felt that being sexually active kind of made me a threat. Why? Well, I've heard so many stories from women about men being letches - blokes who wolf-whistle, cat-call and are generally pricks on account of their dicks. When I heard those stories, I felt like I was on the losing team, one of the bad guys, another bloke who thought only with his meat popsicle. For example, whenever I saw someone who gave me a 'twinge in the trouser department', I'd feel guilty - I was just another slack-jawed, gawping idiot. Even though I wasn't shouting out loud, on the inside I was thinking about how I'd like to do sexy time with that woman, and that's not feminist, is it? Basically, I felt like my sex drive made me objectify women, which is wrong. I didn't want to conform to the stereotype pervert who's 'obsessed by the chest', 'a felon for the melons', 'stumped on account of the lady lumps'. I didn't want to be bam-boob-zled when an attractive girl walked past, but whenever one did, I'd always feel my head swivel in her direction like some pervy owl. It was a battle between my head and my 'part'. As the anorexia numbed me, it also numbed my sex drive - if your brain doesn't have enough energy to release 'the sexy chemicals', then your sex drive drops like soap in a prison shower. And, let me tell you, when you don't have a sex drive, you get much less distracted (you get a lot more admin done when you've no sex drive).

Getting my sex drive back was terrifying - imagine going through puberty...second time round. I mean, at least the first time you have the excuse of being a horny teenager; when you're 25, people think you're having some sort of breakdown. Therapy sparked a big change – I'd always been the anorexic camp guy with no sex drive. Now I was getting my masculinity and libido back, and it made me think, 'Who *even* am I?' (which is normally only the sort of thing you can ask while holding a spliff and a copy of Descartes). Getting my libido back made me weak to sexual temptation and that made me vulnerable – one of the other things I enjoyed about not having a sex drive was avoiding sexual politics. If you don't want sex, then you're not burnt by rejection on nights out, at parties and places where people hook up.

There's also another reason I was so scared – I always found sex painful. It's a long story, but through the process of therapy I realised I needed to have a circumcision as I had a thing called phimosis (which basically means the 'neck' on my 'jumper' was a little bit too tight...if you catch my drift?). That made sex incredibly painful (however, having it cut off was hardly a picnic either). The pain made me even more scared of sex, which was a bit of a mindfuck – because I wanted sex, but I was scared to have it, as it was bloody painful. Now can you see why I'm such a screw-up?

I learnt this and so much more. But, this isn't *Dave's Therapy Diaries*. All you need to know is that therapy was tough but genuinely good fun. And it also leads me to the last part of the story.

TIPS TO HELP AT THIS STAGE

Reading other people's experiences

It's easy to think that what's happening to you has never happened to anyone ever before. Most of the time that isn't true. In fact, just a bit of research will show that whatever you are going through – good, bad or indifferent – has been experienced by someone else who has tried to explain it. This doesn't have to be an eating disorder, or even something negative. It could be anything. Sometimes just knowing you're not alone can be all it takes. Two heads are better than one. Sometimes other people's experiences can hold up a mirror to your own and make things a little clearer with the distance of perspective. YouTube, Podcasts and Google are amazing places to start if you want to feel less alone in whatever you're going through.

Antidepressants

I'm not saying you have to get drugged up to the eyeballs in order to function, but being put on a low dose of antidepressants when I had my blip made a noticeable and quick difference. You wouldn't mind taking tablets if you were diabetic and not releasing insulin; you don't have to mind taking them if your brain's not releasing enough serotonin.

Taking things less seriously
I found something really odd – when I get depressed, I become all angry and incredibly grumpy. Learning to spot this has been really helpful, but it's also a good example of changing behaviours. Now, I have to make a conscious choice to find the funny in things rather than getting annoyed. After all, laughing is more enjoyable than shouting. This is one personal example, and maybe there's something out there for you – a problem and a 'fun' solution (or you might think this one's a bit wanky and a bit shit).

Enjoying it
Personally I don't think that mental health should be boring. Surely good mental health is bitchin'. Creativity, fun and humour have helped me to make sense of what's in my head, and that's helped me deal with the good, bad and plain weird.

Out of office
With smartphones, laptops and 24-hour facilities, it's easy to feel that you should always be working. Being accessible all day, every day, makes me anxious that I'm missing

out. One of the things that's helped me is finding a time when I don't need my phone (and I'm not expecting any calls). I'll switch it off and put my out of office on. That helps relieve my anxiety and helps me 'be in the moment'. Sometimes taking a break from the electronic attachment at the end of your arm can actually help put things into perspective.

Section 6

MAINTENANCE

SONGS FOR THIS SECTION

Baz Luhrmann – Everybody's Free to Wear Sunscreen
Yeti – Never Lose Your Sense of Wonder
The Libertines – Don't Look Back into the Sun
Rusted Root – Send Me on My Way
Jamiroquai – Virtual Insanity
Pharrell Williams – Happy
Clean Bandit – Symphony
The Avalanches – Frontier Psychiatrist
Oasis – Don't Look Back in Anger
Yellowcard – Believe
Bright Eyes – First Day of My Life
Green Day – Good Riddance
Milky Chance – Stolen Dance
Daughter – Youth
James – Getting Away with It
David Bowie – Heroes
Lord Huron – The Night We Met
Mike Posner – Cooler Than Me
Paramore – The Only Exception
Kygo – Firestone
The Coral – Pass It On
Edward Sharpe and the Magnetic Zeros – Home

It's hard to tie this all up with a nice neat little ending like *Cinderella*, *Sleeping Beauty* or *Grand Designs* (I still love that show). I can't do a 'Happily Ever After' butterflies-and-rainbows-type ending because it isn't that easy. I'd love to leave you feeling all warm and fuzzy as if you'd just been hugged by Santa, the Easter Bunny and the Tooth Fairy all at once but, you know what, life isn't like that. Being balls-to-the-wall truthful with you, I'm not done with recovery. I think it's something you get better at, rather than 'finish'. So I've compromised the chintzy Oprah Winfrey ending in order to be honest with you (because I feel we're friends now).

This is the part where things start all over again. Life after Eating Disorders. It's about finding new, healthier and better ways to cope beyond anorexia. It's about understanding the past in order to try to change things in the future. Sounds like a

> **'Maintenance'**
> * A fresh start – practising new behaviours and ways of thinking
> * Understanding – implementing things to avoid relapsing and safely revisit potential triggers to get rid of them and prepare coping strategies
> * Longevity – re-evaluating your progress to stay on track

pretty big task, doesn't it? Well, being honest, it is. And that's why this one can't be wrapped up with the words 'and they lived happily ever after'.

In many ways this is the least sexy section. Whenever

you read about eating disorders, you'll probably hear people's lowest point, lowest weight, how it began and maybe how they 'recovered'. But I don't think I've ever seen much on how to *stay* in 'recovery'.

Understanding why I turned to anorexia helped me. You can't fix something unless you know how it works in the first place. A lot of the stuff that was going on wasn't conscious – I didn't start out trying to be anorexic. Getting an understanding of why I turned to restriction, calorie counting and weighing helped break that cycle. For me, anorexia meant different things at different times. So let's massively oversimplify this shit:

STAGE: PRECONTEMPLATION – AGED 17

Explanation
I'd been happy growing up. Things were perfect. That was coming to an end and everything began changing. I didn't know how to deal with it.

Reason
Restriction helped numb confusing emotions.
Weighing was a promise things would get better if I lost more.
Exercise gave me an outlet for my frustration.

STAGE: CONTEMPLATION – AGED 19

Explanation
I moved to uni and didn't know anyone, anything or anywhere. That increased the undercurrent of loneliness I'd always had.
Oh yeah, and also Dad nearly died.

Reason
Restriction felt nostalgic and was a shot of homeliness when I needed it.
Weighing felt like I had a grip on something.
Exercise made me feel like I was in charge of something

↓

STAGE: PREPARATION – AGED 19–23

Explanation
I moved to London. I got trapped in a job with an asshole boss. I got a new job...and got sacked!

Reason
Restriction was the one consistent thing in my life.
Weighing was a way of proving to myself I could be 'good' at something.
Exercise was a way of getting rid of the guilt from what I'd eaten.

↓

STAGE: RELAPSE - AGED 23-25

Explanation

Even though I'd never recovered (so couldn't really 'relapse'), anorexic traits accelerated. I became a comic full-time and everything was exciting but a bit uncertain.

Reason

Restriction helped explain things weren't OK when I couldn't.

Weighing became an obsessive way of 'measuring' how much control I had.

Exercise helped me (quite literally) feel like I was running away from something.

↓

STAGE: MAINTENANCE - AGED 26...

Explanation

Starting to find healthy ways to cope and life beyond eating disorders.

Reason

Well, it's not really like the anorexia had helped, had it?

Over the years anorexia subtly became a way of getting by. It was consistent, measurable and exciting. It helped 'explain me'. Basically, it took over.

Now, I know that you might be thinking, 'This is all very well and good, Dave, but you haven't oversimplified this incredibly complex psychiatric condition enough,' So, having thought about it I've sort of worked out that for me (and I can't speak for everyone) my anorexia had four main functions:

NUMBNESS

When you don't feed the body, you don't feed the brain. When you don't feed the brain, it starts shutting down. That meant it became a way of 'muting' chaotic, unwanted and unidentifiable emotions. Things like jealousy, self-doubt, my sex drive and all those nasty emotions I was embarrassed to have. Anorexia helped me break from reality and in turn cope with everything. It was a sedative, a dampener and an invisible comfort blanket.

DISTRACTION

If I could focus on calories, exercise and weighing, I believed everything would sort itself out. It dealt in numbers, figures and facts, so it was a good way to measure how well I was doing at something (which in most aspects of life is pretty rare). Better still, it was something I had power over. It was an obsession that felt 'above' life, more important than anything else.

IDENTITY

I'd never been cool, sporty or geeky. I never had a one-word identity label, something that could explain who I was. The term 'anorexic' became my description. I wanted something to define me because I couldn't define myself. Restriction, exercise and calorie counting was a sort of anchor, something constant that didn't change like emotions, moods or age.

EXPLANATION

I used my body to try to explain there was something wrong with my mind. It was a way to show something was wrong even though I couldn't describe it. I've never had the tools to express emotions and I felt self-indulgent trying to offload all my shit on to other people (who all had their own baggage).

I suppose the big question is: what do you do about it? That's why I've tried to include things that might be helpful in each of the different sections, but that's nowhere near oversimplified enough for me. So here's a handful of places that are a basic place to start:

KNOW YOUR TRIGGERS

This one's a good starting point. I've always loved the phrase 'nip it in the bud' – not only because it's fun to say (try saying it as fast as you can and I guarantee you'll chuckle) but because it makes a lot of sense. If you find the root of the problem, everything else falls into place. That doesn't even have to be an eating disorder or any mental health issue – if you go straight to the source of the issue, you save yourself a lot of work. So think about what sets you off. If something creates an uncomfortable spark in your mind that you can't explain, make a note of it, forget it at the time and try to revisit it later to understand what might've been going on. You may not find the answers overnight, it might take a bit of untangling, but believe me, if you take time to find out your triggers, your future self will thank you.

KNOW YOUR WARNING SIGNS

Sounds similar, but it's different. Sometimes you might not realise you're a bit wonky in the upstairs department... which isn't that odd when you think about it. You wouldn't know your boiler is dodgy until it blows up or breaks down. A lot of the time it's the same with mental health. But that doesn't mean you should wait to get ill before you can get better. Prevention's better than cure, and stopping a problem developing is a lot easier than dealing with one that already has. Try to find out what your warning signs are. A good place to start is a 'Mood Diary'. Basically, this is where you measure your mood on a numbered scale and track it throughout the day. This helps pick up patterns of things you might be unaware of, which boost or kill your mood, so you can avoid triggers. It's a great way to make you feel more in control and optimistic for change.

RECOVERY GOALS

It's hard to accomplish something when you don't know what you're meant to be achieving. Give yourself manageable goals you can hit. That way, you can feel like you're making progress and can congratulate yourself once you get there. For example, one of my personal goals was to go for a coffee and a croissant with my mates. It sounds pathetic (and maybe it is), but doing that without belly pinching, calorie counting, obsessing and freaking out made my 'recovery' something enjoyable rather than annoying.

EAT REGULARLY

This one really helped me. There's a fine line between disordered eating and an eating disorder. Getting into bad habits probably won't help you. On the flip side, getting into good habits probably will. It sounds ridiculous, but eating at roughly the same time every day helped stop me binging – it's easier to build up a routine when it's done roughly at the same time every day. Once I did that, it reduced my desire to purge and helped regulate my eating. Simples!

REPETITION

Don't forget, anorexia doesn't develop overnight, so it probably won't go away in a matter of hours either. It might take time to break free of it. Now, that might sound bleak, but it isn't when you really think about it – if you had to choose between a positive thought process and a negative one, the positive one probably holds a more exciting future.

ALLOW YOURSELF THE ODD FUCK-UP

Following on from that, this one's important, too. You'll probably screw up every now and then. Personally, I think that's part of recovery – sometimes you have to push the boundaries to know they're there at all. So, don't beat yourself up if you have the odd 'off day'. No one's perfect and, you know what, no one should want to be. If you do fuck up, as long as you learn from it, and try to make sure it doesn't happen again, then (in the words of Elsa) let it go.

ENJOY IT

I get annoyed when everything about 'recovery' seems dull. It shouldn't be. I decided to treat recovery as my new 'project' to make it fun rather than boring. For me, anorexia was a short-term distraction – like booze or drugs. There are positive and negative methods of distraction. 'Recovery' is about finding the positive ones to distract, explain and help you. It's not about the person you want to be, but the person you are. Try something new, something exciting, something different. This could be personality tests, playing a musical instrument, baking or scrapbooking. In fact, that's something I'm doing at the moment. I've got a drawer filled with ticket stubs, festival passes, old posters, flyers and photos. I'm trying to organise this so that when things get a little full-on I have somewhere to go for a little pick-me-up to remind me that everything isn't always shit. Whatever you do, make sure you enjoy it – no one wants this process to be shit, believe me!

UNDERSTAND HOW OTHER PEOPLE CAN HELP
Whenever people say you should 'just talk', it pisses me off. That makes it sound easy, like I must understand all of this stuff. It's also pretty naive. If I meet up with a mate for a coffee, I don't want to treat him/her as my personal unpaid therapist! I don't want to offload all of my shit on to them so they'll dread ever getting a text from me again. That's why I think it's important to think about what other people can help you with *but also* what you can help them with. It doesn't have to be all about taking; it can be about giving as well (*snigger*). It might be something like having a gaming night once a month or going to the cinema – something that you both get something out of.

BE HONEST WITH YOURSELF
Yup, this is perhaps the hardest of the lot. Sometimes the hardest person to be truthful with is yourself. No one can make you engage with treatment, it has to come from you.

That doesn't mean you're alone – there's tonnes of help out there. But it does mean that you have to start being honest with yourself. Sometimes the most uncomfortable thoughts can be the most important ones. Only when you realise/acknowledge that there's a problem can you begin to deal with it.

All this oversimplification aside, it's important to point out that everyone's different so everyone's 'recovery' is different. It took me two and a half years before I was discharged from therapy. I'd never really thought about what it'd be like to leave therapy. Don't get me wrong, I didn't expect a trumpet fanfare or red-carpet treatment. However, my last session was almost mundanely routine. My therapist told me this was going to be the last meeting and gave me info for where to go if ever I needed help again. It was like a break-up where you stay friends. There was no drama or ceremony; that was just it – things had run their course and we were done. But that's life, I guess. If this'd been a movie, then it'd finish with me (played by Eddie Redmayne) on the steps of the Maudsley with the rain slowly trickling down while some violins and that start playing. There'd be the odd close-up of tears running down my (well, Eddie's) cheek, and a prophetic voice-over going:

> If I learnt one thing, it's that you can't sum up life in just one sentence. No one's perfect, and no one

should want to be. It's our little imperfections that make us who we are – different, unique and brilliant. Everyone's running from something. It doesn't have to be an eating disorder; it doesn't even have to be a mental illness – everyone has a shadow they're trying to lose. But it's not about running away from the darkness; it's about aiming towards the light. We're all on a journey and sometimes there's the odd diversion. It's important that doesn't knock you off track. Because, at the end of the day, it's not about where you've come from; it's about where you're heading.

Then the clouds would part, the sun would break through and 'Never Lose Your Sense of Wonder' by Yeti would start playing (if you haven't heard that song, seriously, check it out). He'd smirk, get up and walk out of shot while the credits begin to roll. All the audience would start clapping (even though it's a film, not the theatre) and there wouldn't be a dry eye in the house.

But this isn't Hollywood, and I'm not Eddie Redmayne. 'Recovery' takes time, and in the end it's not something you 'finish'. In that respect, physical health and mental health aren't too different – you have to keep on top of them and it takes hard work, time and persistence. But in the long run it's well worth it. 'Recovery' is something you have to do for yourself – nobody can do it for you. And keeping healthy (both mentally and physically) will mean different things at different times of life, so it's something you've got to keep an eye on.

I hope you don't find this dispiriting. But the non-Eddie Redmayne version of me is a lot blunter. I think it's important to be truthful, so that if you're in recovery (or heading towards it), you can be better prepped than I was. There might be a couple of speed bumps along the way, and I want you to expect that rather than think everything's falling apart, because it probably isn't. And, being honest, even while writing this I had a bit of a blip. I began getting depressed again without realising; I began getting sapped of energy, enjoyment and interest in anything. I became angry, frustrated and anxious; I lost my concentration, patience and perspective. (It didn't help that I had a bloody book to write and that's a shit-tonne of work by the way! You think *War and Peace* is hard to read – you have a go at writing the bloody thing.) All the things I'd been writing about had begun to happen again but I didn't realise. I was too wrapped up in the here-and-now to zoom out and recognise that things had gone a bit askew. It took me months to realise I needed to go to the doctor and nearly as long to accept it. Going on antidepressants again felt like a step back. But I did, and part of the process of 'recovery' is learning to spot the signs that things might not be right and find ways to steer things back on track.

So, as we're getting nearer and nearer the ending, it gets

harder and harder to wrap this up with a neat little bow. I could lie and give you the Happily Ever After version, but it'd be dishonest and I don't want to lie to you. I'm not trying to pretend I have all of the answers. 'Recovery' changes over time, so of course there's going to be the odd surprise along the way...

But that doesn't always have to be a bad thing. For example, I met my girlfriend through all this. She's a doctor of psychology and did her thesis on men with eating disorders. She'd seen my TED Talk, got in touch and we began emailing. Months later we met at a conference in Brighton where she was presenting her research and I was hosting. We hit it off, swapped numbers and went on a couple of dates. I wasn't really her boyfriend, more of a case study! It's been two and a half years now and we're living together in a pokey little flat in South London - just her, me and her gazillion stuffed toys. And I don't think the sound of church bells are too far off, so - who knows? - in the next couple of years you might have to buy a big hat!

But this isn't *Romeo and Juliet* and I'm certainly not Bill Shakespeare. I'm certainly not a professional either, so I don't have all of the answers. I hope this has been helpful to make you think, give you some ideas where to start and to come up with ways to keep yourself mentally healthy. 'Recovery' doesn't have to be about losing anything - it's about finding ways to get back on top, back in control and able to cope healthily. Good mental health isn't an end goal;

it's a starting point and one where things can become fun, funny and enjoyable. I hope you get there.

Thank you so much for reading. If you've enjoyed the book, please recommend it to other people. Honestly, word-of-mouth is better than any advertising and I've tried to keep it as cheap as possible so it doesn't break the bank to buy it and the people that need it have access to it. If you've enjoyed it, please share the word; if you've enjoyed it, please pass it on (if you haven't, please keep schtum!). If you'd like to come and see me live, all my gig dates are on my website – www.DaveChawner.co.uk or you could follow me on Twitter @DaveChawner.

If you'd like more help for eating disorders, Beat (the UK's eating disorder charity) have helplines, chat services and online support. Their website is www.beateatingdisorders.org.uk. If you're a bloke and would like more info on men with eating disorders, I'm a proud ambassador of a charity called Men Get Eating Disorders Too. Their website is www.mengetedstoo.co.uk.

If you'd like more info on mental health, Mind is a great place to start. They're on www.mind.org.uk. Also, you've got the Mental Health Foundation which can be found at www.mentalhealth.org.uk and MQ which lives at www.mqmentalhealth.org.

Finally, you've got the Samaritans. I've used them a number of times and I think they're brilliant. They're open 24/7 for confidential chats; you just have to give them a buzz. Check out their website – www.samaritans.org.

If you are worried about yourself, or anyone else, don't worry: there is help out there. Go to a GP, talk to someone you trust and take your time – it might take time to understand, but it's well worth it if you do. Good luck!

www.beateatingdisorders.org.uk
www.mengetedstoo.co.uk
www.mind.org.uk
www.mentalhealth.org.uk
www.mqmentalhealth.org
www.samaritans.org

...and for absolutely no help at all
www.DaveChawner.co.uk!